ASIAN
VEGETARIAN
FEAST

ASIAN VEGETARIAN FEAST

KEN·HOM

TEMPTING

VEGETABLE &

PASTA RECIPES

FROM THE EAST

QUILL
WILLIAM MORROW
NEW YORK

To Madhur Jaffrey
A superb cook and good friend
Your natural elegance is an inspiration.

Portions of this book first appeared as *Ken Hom's Vegetable and Pasta Book* which was published in Great Britain by BBC Books. This edition is published by arrangement with BBC Books, a division of BBC Enterprises, Ltd., London, England.

Library of Congress Cataloging-in-Publication Data

Hom, Ken.
   Asian vegetarian feast : tempting vegetable and pasta
recipes from the East / Ken Hom.
      p.   cm.
   ISBN 0-688-15138-8 (pbk.)
   1. Cookery (Vegetables)   2. Cookery (Pasta)   3. Cookery, Oriental.
I. Title.
[TX801.H66   1997]
641.5'636'095—dc20   96-26421
                                                              CIP

Printed in the United States of America

First Quill Edition

1   2   3   4   5   6   7   8   9   10

BOOK DESIGN BY LINEY LI

ART BY JANIE PAUL

Acknowledgments

Any cookbook requires meticulous attention to detail, and it is almost impossible for the author, without the help of others, to do everything that must be done to make it as useful and interesting as possible. This book is no exception. I owe an immense debt to Gordon Wing, who is a great chef in his own right. His unerring good taste and expert working and testing of the recipes helped ensure their accuracy. I am grateful to Mimi Luebbermann for her considerable editorial skills and talents of organization. Her vast experience and many useful suggestions helped make this a better book. In addition, her precise copyediting was invaluable. My deep thanks and appreciation go to Gerry Cavanaugh, whose skillful research and editing helped me to clarify my thoughts and to present them precisely.

I am grateful to my wonderful editor, Ann Bramson, and to assistant editor Mark Jockers for shepherding this book through the publishing process and for their enthusiasm.

Credit should go also to Liney Li for the design of the book and to Victor Budnick for his superb jacket photograph.

And for playing no small part in this book and in all of my professional activities, my special thanks to Ted Lyman, my international agent, and Martha Casselman, my literary agent. Their sound advice and good sense have been of incalculable benefit to me over the years, and they have my deep appreciation.

Contents

Introduction

Meatless cooking is the subject of this book for two reasons. The first is that, growing up within the Chinese culinary tradition, fresh vegetables, pasta, rice, and bean curd—wonderful foods!—have been central to my diet, to my personal and professional life, since I can remember. I am not a vegetarian. However, my diet does consist primarily of vegetables, pasta, and seafood, with poultry and meat quite secondary and always in small portions. The second reason is that one of the most exciting culinary developments in Western cuisine has been the recent introduction of the whole range of Eastern foods and ingredients. Vegetables that used to be unknown or considered strange are now readily available in American produce stores and supermarkets. "Pasta" now encompasses Asian versions of that universally enjoyed food—Chinese rice noodles, Vietnamese rice papers, Japanese udon and buckwheat noodles. Flavors rarely experienced, such as lemongrass and Sichuan peppercorns, are now well on their way to becoming standards in homecooked meals.

Thus Spicy Korean Kimchi, with its garlic, ginger, green onions, and dried chili, and Fiery Sichuan Soup, with its jolting seasonings, have won the hearts and flameproof palates of American lovers of "hot" foods. Now we crave the crispy sweet-and-sour spiciness of Chinese pickled cabbage or Crunchy Radish Salad. We want the brightness of recipes like Rainbow Vegetables in Lettuce Cups. Pasta dishes such as Crispy Cantonese-style Noodles with Vegetables, aromatic Tan-Tan Noodles, and subtle Singapore-style Rice Noodles are already popular favorites, and Japanese and Indonesian soups grace our tables. What was once Asian and exotic has become American and familiar.

Most of the recipes in this collection derive from my Chinese culinary tradition, the basis of my own style. Many of them can accompany other dishes, Asian or non-Asian, vegetarian or not, luncheon, dinner, or supper. The recipes embody ideas, flavors, colors, aromas, textures, and esthetics derived from my dual Asian-Western heritage. They are authentically Asian but reflect as well my own tastes and experiences, as for example, the crunchy surprise of stir-fried cucumbers.

I have arranged the recipes in the usual order: appetizers to desserts. Please note that some appetizers and soups may serve as meals in themselves, some cold dishes make admirable side courses in complete meals. There is a chapter each on hot pasta and noodles and cold pasta and noodles. I have devoted separate chapters to bean curd dishes and rice, the two great staples of Chinese and other Asian cuisines. Bean curd, or tofu, is becoming increasingly familiar to Americans and for sound nutritional reasons: Low in cholesterol and calories, high in protein, an adaptable and congenial food, bean curd is close to being the ideal ingredient for almost any substantial dish. Americans who have adopted bean curd into their diets tend, in the manner of converts, perhaps to exaggerate its virtues, great though they are. However, try the Sweet and Sour Bean Curd dish or the Coconut-stewed Bean Curd with Vegetables—maybe, because I am so familiar with it, I myself take its virtues too much for granted.

As for rice, Americans are certainly familiar with it, but I think do not fully understand or take advantage of its potential in their diet. Thus I offer a short introduction to its charms and include some recipes designed to show off its versatility. Start out with, for example, the Thai Aromatic Fried Rice or the Corn and Ginger Fried Rice. They alone will make you pay more attention to this humble/noble food.

If you wish, you may add meat or poultry appropriately to some of the dishes. As for pasta dishes, I agree with the food critic who wrote that the phrase *al dente* is both overworked and vague. The only workable test of doneness for both vegetables and pasta is the "nibble test." Nibble or taste your foods while preparing them; only you can tell when enough is enough.

I have included various recipe lists under different themes—Do-Ahead, Large Crowds, Light and Summery, etc.—to make the book more useful.

Use these recipes so as to make them your own: Experiment with them, play with them. They are not endings but beginnings. I can only guide your first steps into this delightful terrain. Your taste and imagination, with loving care in your preparations, will take you much farther than any guide could ever do. Practice, and change the recipes to make them your own. Happy cooking and good eating!

Ingredients

Fresh vegetables are, of course, essential to good cooking. But equally important are the proper ingredients—the seasonings, spices, and sauces that complement and enhance the virtues of the vegetables. The recipes in this book draw upon a number of special ingredients which give a distinctive taste to the vegetables and pasta, making them authentic versions of the Chinese, Japanese, and Southeast Asian originals.

All the ingredients used in these recipes can be obtained in this country, if not from your local supermarket then certainly from an Asian specialty market. It is well worth the effort to find your nearest Asian specialty market and to build up a stock of the most frequently used ingredients.

One ingredient commonly used, which you will *not* find mentioned here, is the additive monosodium glutamate (also known as MSG, Ve Tsin, Accent, seasoning, or taste powder). This is a white crystalline extract of grains and vegetables widely used to tenderize and enhance the natural flavor of certain foods. Some people experience an adverse reaction to it, suffering symptoms such as headaches, excessive thirst, and heart palpitations. This allergic response is sometimes known as "Chinese restaurant syndrome." I believe that the freshest and finest ingredients need no enhancing, and I therefore never use monosodium glutamate.

Below, I have listed, in alphabetical order, all the special ingredients used in this book. More detailed information on specific vegetables and types of pasta and noodles is given in the introductions to those chapters.

☐ BAMBOO SHOOTS

Bamboo shoots are the young edible shoots of certain kinds of bamboo. In this country, they are available canned and on rare occasions, fresh. Pale yellow with a crunchy texture, they come peeled and either whole or thickly sliced. They can be bought in most supermarkets, delicatessens, and in Asian specialty markets. Rinse them thoroughly before use and transfer any remaining shoots to a jar, cover them with fresh water and keep in the refrigerator. If the water is changed daily, they will keep for up to a week.

☐ BEAN CURD

Bean curd is also known by its Chinese name, "doufu," or by its Japanese name, "tofu." It has played an important part in Chinese cuisine for over a thousand years: It is highly nutritious, being rich in protein, and combines well with other foods. Bean curd has a distinctive texture but a bland taste. It is made from yellow soybeans which are soaked, ground, mixed with water, and then cooked briefly before being solidified. In this country, it is usually sold in two forms, firm cakes or as a thickish custard, but it is also available in several dried forms and fermented. The soft custard-like variety is used for soups and other dishes, while the solid type is used for stir-frying, braising, and poaching. Solid bean curd "cakes" are white in color and are sold in supermarkets, Asian specialty markets, and in many health food shops. They are packed in water in plastic containers and may be kept in this state in the refrigerator for up to 5 days, providing the water is changed daily. To use solid bean curd, cut the amount required into cubes or shreds using a sharp knife. Do this with care as it is delicate. Bean curd also needs to be cooked carefully as too much stirring can cause it to disintegrate.

Fermented bean curd

Fermented bean curd is a cheese-like form of bean curd preserved in rice wine, and brine with rice or chilies and sold in glass jars at Asian specialty markets. It is used as a flavoring agent, especially for vegetables. A little can add zest to any vegetable dish. Once it begins to cook, it produces a fragrant odor that enriches vegetables. Fermented bean curd comes in several forms: the red fermented bean curd has been cured in a brine with red rice, the chili one has flecks of crushed chilies, and the ordinary one is left plain. Once the jar is opened, it should be stored in the refrigerator, where it will keep well for several months. There is no substitute for this unique ingredient.

Pressed seasoned bean curd

When water is extracted from fresh bean curd cakes by pressing them with a weight, the bean curd becomes firm and compact. Simmered in water with soy sauce, star anise, and sugar, the pressed bean curd acquires a brownish color and smooth, resilient texture. Cut into small pieces, it can be stir-fried with meat or vegetables; and when cut into larger pieces, it can be simmered. In China, pressed bean curd is a popular offering at many food stalls. It can be found in Asian specialty markets. Substitute fresh firm bean curd if it is unavailable.

⊡ BLACK BEANS

These small black soybeans, also known as salted black beans, are preserved by being fermented with salt and spices. They have a distinctive, slightly salty taste and a pleasantly rich smell, and are used as a seasoning, often in conjunction with garlic and fresh ginger. Black beans are inexpensive and can be obtained from Asian specialty markets, usually in cans, as "black beans in salted sauce"; you may also see them packed in plastic bags, which are preferable. Rinse before use; I prefer to chop the beans slightly too. Transfer any unused beans and liquid to a sealed jar and they will keep indefinitely if stored in the refrigerator.

⊡ CHILIES

Chilies are used extensively in western China and somewhat less frequently in the south, as well as many parts of Southeast Asia. They are the seed pods of the capsicum plant and can be obtained fresh, dried, or ground.

Fresh chilies

Fresh chilies can be distinguished by their small size and elongated shape. They should look fresh and bright with no brown patches or black spots. There are several varieties. Red chilies are generally milder than green ones because they sweeten as they ripen.

To prepare fresh chilies, first rinse them in cold water. Using a small sharp knife, slit them lengthways and remove and discard the seeds. Rinse the chilies well under cold running water, and then prepare them according to the instructions in the recipe. Wash your hands, knife, and chopping board before preparing other foods, and be careful not to touch your eyes until you have washed your hands thoroughly with soap and water.

Dried red chilies

Dried red chilies are small and thin, and about ½-inch long. They are used to season oil for stir-fried dishes, sauces, and for braising. Dried chilies are normally left whole or cut in half lengthways and the seeds left in. The Chinese like them to blacken and remain in the dish during cooking, but as they are extremely hot and spicy, you may choose to remove them after using them to flavor the cooking oil. Dried chilies can be found in most supermarkets and in Asian specialty markets, and they will keep indefinitely in a tightly covered jar.

Chili powder

Chili powder, also known as cayenne pepper, is made from dried red chilies. It is pungent, aromatic, and ranges from hot to very hot; it is thus widely used in many spicy dishes. You will be able to buy chili powder in any supermarket.

Chili bean sauce

This is a thick dark sauce or paste made from soybeans, chilies and other seasonings, and is very hot and spicy. Widely used in cooking in western China, it is usually available here in jars in Asian specialty markets. Be sure to seal the jar tightly after use and store in the refrigerator. Do not confuse it with chili sauce (see below) which is a hot, red, thinner sauce made without beans and used mainly as a dipping sauce for cooked dishes. There are Southeast Asian versions of chili bean sauce and I find them very spicy and hot. You can use them if you like, but throughout this book, I have used the Chinese chili bean sauce which is slightly milder.

Chili oil/dipping sauce

2 tablespoons dried red
  chilies, chopped
1 tablespoon unroasted
  Sichuan peppercorns,
  whole
2 tablespoons black beans,
  whole
⅔ cup peanut oil

Heat a frying-pan or wok over a high heat and add the oil and the rest of the ingredients. Continue to cook over a low heat for about 10 minutes. Allow the mixture to cool undisturbed and then pour it into a jar. Let the mixture sit for 2 days, and then strain the oil. It will keep indefinitely.

Chili oil

Chili oil is an essential ingredient in many of the recipes in this book. This is to be expected inasmuch as it is a staple condiment/flavoring throughout Asia. You may purchase it in Asian specialty markets. The Thai and Malaysian versions are especially hot; the Hong Kong, Taiwanese and Chinese versions are a bit milder. Such commercial products are quite acceptable, and I include this recipe only because the homemade version is the best. Remember that chili oil is too dramatic to be used directly in cooking; it is best applied as a final spicy touch. I include the spices (pepper and black beans) for additional flavors because then, I can also use it as a dipping sauce.

Once made, the chili oil can be put in a tightly sealed glass jar and stored in a cool dark place where it will keep for months.

Chili sauce

Chili sauce is a hot, bright red sauce made from chilies, vinegar, sugar, and salt. It is sometimes used for cooking, but it is mainly used as a dipping sauce. There are various brands available in many supermarkets and Asian specialty markets and you should experiment with them until you find the one you like best. If you find it too strong, dilute it with hot water. Do not confuse this sauce with the chili bean sauce mentioned above which is a much thicker, darker sauce used for cooking.

⊡ CINNAMON STICKS/ BARK

Cinnamon sticks are curled, paper-thin pieces of the bark of the cinnamon tree. Chinese cinnamon comes as thicker sticks of this bark. It is highly aromatic and more pungent than the more common cinnamon sticks, but the latter are an adequate substitute. They add a robust taste to braised dishes and are an important ingredient of five spice powder. Store cinnamon sticks or bark in a tightly sealed jar to preserve their aroma and flavor. Ground cinnamon is not a satisfactory substitute.

⊡ COCONUT MILK

1 small coconut
2 cups low-fat milk
6 tablespoons sugar
1 cup low-fat milk

You can make your own coconut milk according to this recipe:

Preheat the oven to 350°F. To prepare the coconut, pierce two of the "eyes" in the shell and drain and discard the liquid inside. Place the drained coconut in the oven for about 20 minutes. If this does not crack the shell, split it by tapping it with a hammer along its line of cleavage until the coconut breaks apart. (Wrap the coconut in a towel while cracking it to prevent the small pieces from flying about.) Remove the white meat with a knife, discarding any of the brown skin.

Cut the coconut into small pieces and place in a medium-sized saucepan. Cover the 2 cups milk and simmer for 10 minutes. Allow to cool, and process in a blender on high speed for 1 minute. Let the coconut stand for 15 minutes, then strain into a bowl. Using the back of a wooden spoon, squeeze all the liquid from the chopped coconut. Return the coconut milk to the pan, add the sugar and remaining milk. Simmer for 5 minutes until the milk thickens. Allow to cool, then refrigerate.

Alternatively, you can use the canned variety. I have found the canned version quite acceptable and a lot less work. Look for the ones from Thailand or Malaysia. You can find them in Asian specialty markets, usually in 14 fl oz or 15 fl oz cans. Shake the cans well before opening to use. If you are using canned milk, any remainder can be kept in the refrigerator for at least a week in a sealed glass jar.

⊡ **CORIANDER (CHINESE PARSLEY)**

Fresh coriander is one of the relatively few herbs used in Asian cookery. It looks like flat parsley but its pungent, musky, citrus-like flavor gives it a distinctive and unmistakable character. Its feathery leaves are often used as a garnish or it can be chopped and then mixed into sauces and stuffings. Parsley may be used as a substitute but, for an authentic Asian flavor, it is well worth trying to obtain the real thing. Many Asian specialty stores stock fresh coriander, as do some supermarkets. When buying fresh coriander, look for deep green, fresh-looking leaves. Yellow and limp leaves indicate age and should be avoided.

To store coriander, wash it in cold water, drain thoroughly, and put it in a clean plastic bag with a couple of sheets of moist paper towel. Stored in the vegetable compartment of your refrigerator, it should keep for several days.

⊡ CORNSTARCH

In China and Asia, there are many flours and types of starch, such as water chestnut powder, taro starch, and arrowroot, which are used to bind and thicken sauces and to make batter. These exotic starches and flours are difficult to obtain, but I have found cornstarch works just as well in my recipes. As part of a marinade, it helps to coat the food properly and gives dishes a velvety texture. Cornstarch also protects food during deep-frying by helping to seal in the juices, and it can be used as a binder for ground stuffings. Cornstarch is invariably blended with cold water until it forms a smooth paste before it is used in sauces.

⊡ DASHI

Dashi is a clear stock made from dried bonito (tuna) flakes and sea-weed. This is the basis for most Japanese soups. You can make dashi by purchasing the dried bonita flakes and simmering it in water, or you can purchase instant dashi from stores selling Japanese food products. Simply follow the instructions on the package. I have found the instant dashi quite acceptable. Make up only enough to use at the time.

⊡ FIVE SPICE POWDER

Five spice powder is less commonly known as five-flavored powder or five fragrance spice powder, and is available in many supermarkets (in the spice section) and in Chinese grocers. This brownish powder is a mixture of star anise, Sichuan peppercorns, fennel, cloves, and cinnamon. A good blend is pungent, fragrant, spicy, and slightly sweet at the same time. The exotic fragrance it gives to a dish makes the search for a good mixture well worth the effort. It keeps indefinitely in a well sealed jar.

⊡ FLOURS

Glutinous rice flour

This flour is made from glutinous rice and is often used in making pastries to give the chewy texture to the doughs. Available from Asian specialty markets, this is not an acceptable substitute for rice flour.

Rice flour

This flour is made from raw rice and is used to make fresh rice noodles. Obtainable from Asian specialty markets, it is stored as plain flour.

⊡ **FUNGUS**

(see Mushrooms, Chinese Dried)

⊡ **GARLIC**

Garlic has been an essential seasoning in Asian cooking for thousands of years. It would be inconceivable to cook without the distinctive, highly aromatic smell and taste of garlic. Throughout Asia it is used in numerous ways: whole, finely chopped, crushed, and pickled. It is used to flavor oils as well as spicy sauces, and is often paired with other equally pungent ingredients such as scallions, black beans, curry, fish sauce, or fresh ginger.

Select fresh garlic which is firm and preferably pinkish in color. It should be stored in a cool, dry place but not in the refrigerator where it can easily become mildewed or begin sprouting.

⊡ **GINGER**

Fresh root ginger (actually a rhizome, not a root) is indispensable in Asian cooking. Its pungent, spicy, and fresh taste adds a subtle but distinctive flavor to soups, meats, fish, sauces, and vegetables. Fresh ginger looks rather like a gnarled Jerusalem artichoke and can range in size from 3-inches to 6-inches long. It has pale brown, dry skin which is usually peeled away before use. Select fresh ginger which is firm with no signs of shrivelling. It will keep in the refrigerator, well wrapped in plastic wrap, for up to 2 weeks. Fresh ginger can now be found at many produce stores, supermarkets, and in most Asian specialty markets. Dried powdered ginger has a quite different flavor and cannot be substituted for fresh ginger.

Ginger juice

Ginger juice is made from fresh ginger and is used in cooking to give a subtle ginger taste without the bite of the chopped fresh pieces. To make ginger juice, simply take a piece of fresh ginger and smash it with a kitchen mallet or the side of a cleaver or knife until most of the fibers are exposed. Then, with a garlic press or your hands, simply squeeze out the juice. The left-over ginger can be used to flavor the oil before you cook. The fresh ginger juice must be used immediately.

⊡ LEMONGRASS

This aromatic lemony tropical grass is widely used in Southeast Asian cooking and is found in Asian specialty markets. Look for pale green tops and make sure the lemongrass is not dried out. Cut off the fibrous base and peel away the outside layers. Cut off the tops and save to flavor oils or soups. Lemon juice or lemon zest can be used as a substitute. Lemongrass can be sliced and frozen for further use.

⊡ LILY BUDS

Also known as tiger lily buds, golden needles, or lily stems, dried lily buds (*Lilium Lancifolium*) are an ingredient in Mu Shu dishes and hot and sour soups. They add more texture than taste. Soak the buds in hot water for about 30 minutes or until soft. Cut off the hard ends and shred or cut in half according to the recipe.

⊡ MUSHROOMS, CHINESE DRIED

There are many varieties of these which add a particular flavor and aroma to Chinese dishes. These mushrooms can be black or brown in color. The very large ones, with a lighter color and a highly cracked surface, are the best and so they are usually the most expensive. They can be bought in boxes or plastic from Asian specialty markets, and are fairly expensive. Keep them stored in an air-tight jar in a cool dry place.

To use Chinese dried mushrooms

Soak the required amount in hot water for about 20 minutes until soft. Squeeze out any excess liquid and remove the tough, inedible stalk. The mushrooms are now ready for use. The resulting liquid can be used for cooking rice—simply pour off the liquid gently, leaving any sand or residue at the bottom.

Chinese dried cloud ears (black fungus)

These tiny black dried mushrooms are also known as cloud ears because when soaked, they look like little small clouds. Soak the cloud ears in hot water for 20 to 30 minutes until soft. Rinse well and cut away any hard pieces. They are valued for their crunchy texture and slightly smoky flavor. There is some medical research that indicates they are of value in the prevention of heart disease. You can find cloud ears at Asian specialty markets, usually wrapped in plastic or cellophane bags. They keep indefinitely in a jar stored in a cool dry place.

Chinese dried wood ears

These mushrooms are the larger variety of cloud ears. Prepare and soak them in the same way, then rinse well. Once soaked, they will swell up to four or five times their size. Cut away any hard pieces. Sold in Asian specialty markets, they keep indefinitely when stored in a cool dry place.

☐ **NORI**

(see Seaweed)

☐ **OILS**

Oil is the most commonly used cooking medium in Asia. The favorite is peanut oil. Animal fats, usually lard and chicken fat, are also used in some areas, particularly in Indonesia, parts of China. I always prefer to use oil since I find animal fats too heavy.

I find oils are best re-used just once, and this is healthier since constantly re-used oils increase in saturated fat content. To prepare oil for re-use, simply cool the oil after use and filter it through cheesecloth or a fine strainer into a jar. Cover tightly and keep in a cool, dry place. If you keep oil in the refrigerator, it will become cloudy, but it clarifies again at room temperature.

Peanut oil

I prefer to use this for any type of Asian cookery because it has a pleasant, mild taste which is unobtrusive. Although it has a higher saturated fat content than some oils, its ability to be heated to a high temperature makes it perfect for stir-frying and deep-frying. Many supermarkets stock peanut oil, but if you cannot find it use corn oil instead.

Corn oil

Corn oil is also quite suitable for cooking. It has a high heating point although I find it rather bland with a slightly disagreeable smell. Corn oil is high in polyunsaturates and is therefore one of the healthier oils.

Other vegetable oils

Some of the cheaper vegetable oils available include soybean, safflower, and sunflower oils. They are light in color and taste and can also be used in cooking.

Sesame oil

Chinese sesame oil is a thick, rich, golden brown oil made from sesame seeds, which has a distinctive, nutty flavor and aroma. It is widely used in Asian cooking as a seasoning, but is not normally used as a cooking oil because it heats rapidly and burns easily. It is often added at the last moment to finish a dish. It is sold in bottles in many supermarkets and in Asian specialty markets.

⊡ **PEANUTS**

Raw peanuts are used in Asian cooking to add flavor and a crunchy texture and are especially popular in Southeast Asian cooking. They can be bought at health food shops, good supermarkets and Asian specialty markets. The thin red skins need to be removed before you use the nuts. To do this simply, immerse them in a pot of boiling water for about 2 minutes. Drain them, let them cool, and the skins will come off easily.

⊡ **RED IN SNOW**

This is Chinese pickled cabbage that can be bought in cans in Asian specialty markets. It adds a pungent, slightly sour taste to dishes and an interestingly textured vegetable in stir-fry dishes.

⊡ RICE WINE

This wine is used extensively for cooking and drinking throughout China and the finest variety is believed to be that from Shaoxing in Zhejiang Province in eastern China. It is made from glutinous rice, yeast, and spring water. Available from Asian specialty markets, it should be kept at room temperature, tightly corked. A good quality, dry pale sherry can be substituted but cannot equal the rich, mellow taste of Chinese rice wine. Do not confuse this with sake which is the Japanese version of rice wine and quite different. Rice wine can be found at Asian specialty markets.

⊡ SAKE

Sake is a Japanese rice wine often used in Japanese cooking. It should not be confused with Mirin which is a much sweeter wine and cannot be used as a substitute. The more expensive brands are served gently warmed as a drink, but less expensive brands are suitable for cooking. If you do not like the alcohol taste, briefly bring the sake to a boil before it is combined with the other ingredients.

⊡ SAUCES AND PASTES

Asian cookery involves a number of thick tasty sauces or pastes. They are essential to the authentic taste of the food and it is well worth making the effort to obtain them. Most are sold in bottles or cans in Asian specialty markets and some supermarkets. Canned sauces, once opened, should be transferred to screw-top glass jars and kept in the refrigerator where they will last for a long time.

Curry paste

This prepared paste has a stronger curry flavor than the powdered variety. The spices are mixed with oil and chilies. Be sure to get the Indian variety which is generally the best. You can find it at Asian specialty markets. Kept refrigerated after opening, the curry paste keeps indefinitely.

Dipping sauces and mixtures

Many Chinese and Southeast dishes and snacks are dipped into a variety of dipping sauces before being eaten. The most popular of these are chilli sauce, which can be bought ready-made, and Chilli Oil, which can easily be made at home. Soy sauce and red and black Chinese rice vinegars are also widely used as dips. The recipes for dipping sauces accompany each dish but can be easily used with different recipes as you choose. Look in the index under dipping sauces.

Fish sauce

Fish sauce, also known as fish gravy or nam pla, is a thin brownish sauce made from the fermentation of salted fresh fish. It is sold bottled and has a very fishy odor and salty taste. Cooking greatly diminishes the "fishy" flavor and the sauce adds a subtle taste to many dishes. You can find it at Asian specialty markets.

Hoisin sauce

This is a thick, dark, brownish red sauce which is made from soybeans, vinegar, sugar, spices, and other flavorings. It is sweet and spicy and is widely used in southern Chinese cookery. In the West, it is often used as a sauce for Peking Duck instead of the traditional sweet bean sauce. Hoisin sauce, sometimes called barbecue sauce, is sold in cans and jars, and is available in Asian specialty markets and some supermarkets. If refrigerated, it should keep indefinitely.

Oyster sauce

This thick brown sauce is made from a concentrate of oysters cooked in soy sauce and brine. Despite its name, oyster sauce does not taste fishy. It has a rich flavor and is used not only in cooking but as a condiment, diluted with a little oil, for vegetables, poultry, or meats. Oyster sauce is usually sold in bottles and can be bought in Asian specialty markets and some supermarkets. I find it keeps best in the refrigerator.

Sesame paste

This rich, thick, creamy brown paste is made from sesame seeds. It is used in both hot and cold dishes, and is particularly popular in northern and western China. Sesame paste is sold in jars at Asian specialty markets. If you cannot obtain it, use peanut butter.

⊡ SOY SAUCES

Soy sauce is an essential ingredient in Asian cooking. It is made from a mixture of soybeans, flour, and water which is then naturally fermented and matured for some months. The liquid which is finally distilled is soy sauce. There are two main types: light and dark.

Light soy sauce

As the name implies, this is light in color but it is full of flavor and is the best one to use for cooking. It is saltier than dark soy sauce. In Asian specialty markets, light soy sauce is known as Superior Soy.

Dark soy sauce

This sauce is matured for much longer than light soy sauce, hence its darker, almost black color. Slightly thicker and stronger than light soy sauce, it is more suitable for stews. I prefer it to light soy as a dipping sauce. It is known in Chinese grocers as Soy Superior Sauce.

Most soy sauces sold in supermarkets are dark soy. Asian specialty markets sell both types and the quality is superior. Be sure you buy the right one as the names are very similar.

Yellow bean sauce

This thick, spicy, aromatic sauce is made with yellow beans, flour, and salt which are fermented together. It is quite salty but adds a distinctive flavor to Chinese sauces. There are two forms: whole beans in a thick sauce and mashed or puréed beans (sold as crushed yellow bean sauce). I prefer the whole bean because it is slightly less salty and has a better texture. It keeps best in the refrigerator.

☐ **SEAWEED**

Known as nori, seaweed is a nutritious and ancient food. Often used in soups and as a wrapper for sushi, it has a delicate flavor. Nori comes packaged as 10 or more thinly pressed dried sheets. Recipes use different techniques for soaking and cooking. See your recipe for instructions.

☐ **SESAME SEEDS**

These are dried seeds of an Asian annual herb. Unhulled, the seeds range from grayish white to black in color, but once the hull is removed, the sesame seeds are flat, tiny, creamy colored, and pointed on one end. Sesame seeds are valued as a flavoring agent and as a source of oil and paste. Sesame seeds can be found at supermarkets or at Asian specialty markets. Kept in a glass jar in a cool dry place, they will last indefinitely.

To make toasted sesame seeds

Preheat the oven to 325°F. Spread the sesame seeds on a baking tray. Roast them in the oven for about 10 to 15 minutes until they are lightly browned. Allow the toasted seeds to cool, then store them in a glass jar.

☐ **SHERRY**

If you cannot obtain rice wine, you can use a good quality, dry, pale sherry instead. Do not use sweet or cream sherries.

☐ **SHRIMP, DRIED**

Dried shrimp are sold in packets at Asian specialty markets. Look for the brands with the pinkest color and avoid greyish colored ones. They will keep indefinitely stored in a cool dry place. When cooked, the dried shrimp add a delicate taste to sauces unlike the way they smell. The shrimp are sometimes ground to a paste.

☐ **SICHUAN PEPPERCORNS**

Sichuan peppercorns are known throughout China as "flower peppers" because they look like flower buds opening. They are reddish brown in color with a strong pungent odor which distinguishes them from the hotter black peppercorns. Sichuan peppercorns are actually not from peppers at all, but are the dried berries of a shrub which is a member of the citrus family. I find their smell reminds me of lavender, while their taste is sharp and mildly spicy. They can be ground in a conventional peppermill and are very often roasted before grinding to bring out their full flavor. Sold wrapped in cellophane or plastic bags in Asian specialty markets, Sichuan peppercorns are inexpensive. They will keep indefinitely if stored in a well-sealed container.

To roast Sichuan peppercorns

Heat a wok or heavy frying-pan to medium heat. Add the peppercorns (you can cook up to about ⅔ cup at a time) and stir-fry them for about 5 minutes until they brown slightly and start to smoke. Remove the pan from the heat and let cool. Grind the peppercorns in a peppermill, clean coffee grinder, or with a mortar and pestle. Seal the mixture tightly in a screw-top jar to store. Alternatively keep the whole roasted peppercorns in a well sealed container and grind them when required.

☐ **SICHUAN PRESERVED VEGETABLES**

There are many types of Chinese pickled vegetables. One of the most popular is Sichuan preserved vegetable, a specialty of Sichuan Province. This is the root of the mustard green which is pickled in salt and hot chilies. Another type is Sichuan preserved cabbage. Sold in cans in Asian specialty markets, it gives a pleasantly crunchy texture and spicy taste to dishes. Before using the preserved vegetable, rinse in cold water and then slice or chop as required. Any unused vegetables should be transferred to a tightly covered jar and stored in the refrigerator where they will keep indefinitely.

☐ **STAR ANISE**

The star anise is a hard, star-shaped spice and is the seedpod of the anise bush. (It is also known as Chinese anise or whole anise.) It is similar in flavor and fragrance to common aniseed but is more robust and liquorice-like. Star anise is an essential ingredient of five spice powder and is widely used in braised dishes to which it imparts a rich taste and fragrance. Sold in plastic packs in Asian specialty markets, they should be stored in a tightly covered jar in a cool, dry place.

⊡ SUGAR

Sugar has been used in the cooking of savory dishes in China for a thousand years. Properly employed, it helps balance the various flavors of sauces and other dishes. Chinese sugar comes in several forms: as rock or yellow lump sugar, brown sugar slabs, and as maltose or malt sugar. I particularly like to use rock sugar which is rich and has a more subtle flavor than that of refined granulated sugar. It also gives a good lustre or glaze to braised dishes and sauces. You can buy it in Asian specialty markets where it is usually sold in packages. You may need to break the lumps into smaller pieces with a wooden mallet or rolling pin. If you cannot find this, use white sugar or coffee sugar crystals (the amber, chunky kind) instead.

⊡ VINEGARS

Vinegars are widely used in Chinese, Southeast Asian, and Japanese cooking. Unlike Western vinegars they are usually made from rice. There are many varieties, ranging in flavor from the spicy and slightly tart to the sweet and pungent. All these vinegars can be bought in Asian specialty markets. They are sold in bottles and will keep indefinitely. If you cannot obtain Chinese vinegars, I suggest you use cider vinegar instead. Malt vinegar can be used, but its taste is stronger and more acidic.

Black rice vinegar

Black rice vinegar is very dark in color and rich though mild in taste. It is used for braised dishes, noodles, and sauces.

Red rice vinegar

Red rice vinegar is sweet and spicy in taste and is usually used as a dipping sauce for seafood.

White rice vinegar

White rice vinegar is clear and mild in flavor. It has a faint taste of glutinous rice and is used for sweet and sour dishes.

☐ WONTON SKINS

Wonton skins are made from egg and flour and can be bought fresh or frozen from some supermarkets and Asian specialty markets. They are thin pastry-like wrappings which can be stuffed with minced meat, vegetables, or sweet fillings, and fried, steamed, or used in soups. They are sold in little piles of 3 ¼-inch yellowish squares, wrapped in plastic. The number of squares or skins in a packet varies from about 30 to 36, depending upon the supplier. Fresh wonton skins will keep for about 5 days if stored in plastic wrap or a plastic bag in the refrigerator. If you are using frozen wonton skins, just peel off the number you require and thaw thoroughly before you use them.

Equipment

Much of the equipment used in other Asian cooking is similar to the Chinese, so I will discuss traditional Chinese cooking equipment. While not essential for cooking Asian food, there are a few pieces of equipment which will make it very much easier. Most items can be bought very cheaply, especially if you seek out authentic implements from an Asian specialty market, and you can now find fairly good versions sold in many department stores.

The most useful piece of equipment is the wok, in which it is easier to toss foods quickly without spilling them. It also requires far less oil for deep-frying than a deep-fat fryer, although you may find the latter easier and safer to use. Another advantage is that the shape of the wok allows the heat to spread evenly over its surface, thus making for the rapid cooking which is fundamental to stir-frying.

There are two types of wok: the Cantonese wok which has a short, rounded handle on either side, and the pau wok which has one long handle. The Cantonese wok is best for steaming and deep-frying since it can be set steadily onto a stand over the heat, and is easier to move when it is full of liquid. The pau wok is better for stir-frying since it is easier to shake over the heat with one hand while your free hand wields a long-handled spoon or spatula. It also distances you from the heat and hot oil and makes for more comfortable, safer frying. Woks with rounded bases should only be used on gas burners. It is now possible to buy woks with flattish bottoms which are specifically

▣ WOK

designed for electric stove burners but can also be used with gas as well. Although these really defeat the purpose of the traditional design, which is to concentrate intense heat at the center, they do have the advantage of having deeper sides than a frying-pan.

Choosing a wok

Choose a large wok, preferably about 12 to 14 inches in diameter, with good deep sides. Some woks on the market are too shallow and are no better than a large frying-pan. Clearly, it is easier to cook a small quantity in a large wok than to try to accommodate a large quantity in a small one. Select one which is heavy and, if possible, made of carbon steel rather than a light stainless steel or aluminum. The latter types tend to scorch. I do not like non-stick woks; not only are they more expensive, but they also cannot be seasoned like an ordinary wok, and this seasoning adds to the flavor of the food. I also dislike electric woks because I find they do not heat up to a sufficiently high temperature and tend to be too shallow.

Seasoning a wok

All woks (except non-stick ones) need to be seasoned. Many need to be scrubbed first as well to remove the machine oil which is applied to the surface by the manufacturer to protect it in transit. This is the *only* time you will ever scrub your wok unless you let it rust up. Scrub it with an abrasive cleanser and water to remove as much of the machine oil as possible. Then dry it and put it on the stove burner over a low heat. Add 2 tablespoons of cooking oil and rub this over the inside of the wok, using paper towels until the entire surface is lightly coated with oil. Heat the wok slowly for about 10 to 15 minutes, and then wipe it thoroughly with more paper towel. The paper will become blackened. Repeat this process of coating, heating, and wiping until the paper towel wipes clean. Your wok will darken and become well seasoned with use.

Cleaning a wok

Do not scrub a seasoned wok. Just wash it in plain water without detergent. Dry it thoroughly, preferably by putting it over a low heat for a few minutes before storing. This should prevent the wok from rusting, but if it does, scrub the rust off with an abrasive cleanser and repeat the seasoning process.

⊡ **WOK ACCESSORIES**

Wok stand

This is a metal ring or frame designed to keep a conventionally shaped wok steady on the stove burner and is essential if you want to use your wok for steaming, deep-frying, or braising. Stands come in two designs. One is a solid metal ring with about six ventilation holes. The other is like a circular thin wire frame. If you have a gas cooker use only the latter type as the more solid design does not allow for sufficient ventilation and may lead to a build-up of gas which could put the flame out completely.

Wok lid

A wok lid is a dome-like cover, usually made from aluminum, which is used for steaming. It may come with the wok, or it can be purchased separately, but any large domed pan lid which fits snugly over the top of the wok can be used instead. Alternatively, you could use aluminum foil.

Spatula

A long-handled metal spatula shaped rather like a small shovel is ideal for scooping and tossing food in a wok. Any good long-handled spoon can be used instead.

Rack

If you use your wok or a large pan as a steamer, you will need a wooden or metal rack or trivet to stand above the water level and support the plate of food to be steamed. Some woks are sold with a metal stand, but most Asian specialty markets, department stores, and hardware shops stock triangular wooden stands or round metal stands which can be used for this purpose. You can improvise a stand by using an empty, inverted tin can of suitable height.

⊡ **DEEP-FAT FRYERS**

These are very useful, and you may find them safer and easier to use for deep-frying than a wok. *The quantities of oil given in the recipes are based on the amount required for deep-frying in a wok. If you are using a deep-fat fryer instead, you will need about double that amount, but never fill it more than half-full with oil.*

⊡ **CLEAVERS**

No self-respecting Chinese or Southeast Asian cook would be seen with a knife instead of a cleaver. These heavy choppers serve many purposes. They are used for all kinds of cutting, ranging from fine shredding to chopping up bones. A Chinese cook would usually have three types: a lightweight one with a narrow blade for cutting delicate foods including vegetables; a medium-weight one for general cutting, chopping, and crushing purposes; and a heavy one for heavy-duty chopping. Of course, you can prepare Asian food using good sharp knifes, but if you decide to invest in a cleaver, you will be surprised at how easy it is to use. Choose a good quality stainless steel one and keep it sharp.

⊡ **CHOPPING BOARD**

The Chinese traditionally use a soft wood block for chopping, but these blocks are not only difficult to maintain, they also accumulate bacteria. Therefore, I prefer to use a hardwood or acrylic board. Both are strong, easy to clean, and last indefinitely. There is so much chopping and slicing to be done when preparing food for Asian-style cooking that it really is essential to have a large, steady cutting board. (For health reasons, never cut cooked meat on a board which you have also used for chopping raw meat or poultry. Keep a separate board for this purpose.) Always clean your cutting boards properly after use. Vinegar or lemon works well.

⊡ STEAMERS

Bamboo steamers are among the most ancient of Chinese cooking utensils. These attractive round "boxes" come in several sizes of which the 10-inch size is the most suitable for home use. Bamboo steamers are filled with food and placed on top of a pot or over a wok of boiling water. Clean damp cheesecloth is sometimes placed over the open slats under the food to prevent the food from sticking to the steamer. A tight-fitting bamboo lid is put on top to prevent the steam escaping. One of the advantages of the design is that several steamers can be stacked on top of the other for multiple cooking. Bamboo steamers can be bought at Asian specialty markets. (Alternatively, any European kind of wide, metal steamer can be used.) Before using a bamboo steamer for the first time, wash it and steam it empty for about 5 minutes.

⊡ RICE COOKERS

Electric rice cookers are increasing in popularity. They cook rice perfectly and keep it warm throughout a meal. A rice cooker also has the advantage of freeing a burner or element, making for a less cluttered stove top. They are relatively expensive, however, so unless you eat rice frequently, I do not think they are worth the expense.

⊡ SAND OR CLAY POTS

These attractive, lightweight clay pots are also known as sand pots because their unglazed exteriors have a sandy texture. They come in a variety of shapes and sizes equipped with matching lids and sometimes are encased in a wire frame. The pots are designed to be used on the stove top (since most Asians do not have ovens) and are used for braised dishes, soups, and for cooking rice. Never put an empty sand pot on the heat, or put a hot sand pot on a cold surface. In both cases, the pot will crack. Any good casserole or cast-iron pot can be used as a substitute.

⊡ CHOPSTICKS

Chopsticks are not just used for eating in Asian cooking, (with the exception of Thais, who use forks). They are also used when cooking, for stirring, beating, and whipping. Special long chopsticks are available for these purposes, but it is perfectly all right to use Western cooking implements instead.

Table chopsticks come in wood, plastic, and most luxurious of all, ivory or silver. They can be bought at many department stores, Asian specialty markets, and from many Chinese restaurants.

Techniques

The preparation of food before cooking is probably more important and more time-consuming in Chinese, Japanese and Southeast Asian cooking than in any other cuisine. However, because the subject matter of this book is vegetables and pasta, many of the recipes are simpler and easier to make than those dealing with meats and poultry. It is important, nonetheless, to have all ingredients properly prepared beforehand. In stir-frying, for example, the food must be chopped into small, well-shaped pieces. This will ensure even and quick cooking, and is especially important for vegetables to avoid overcooking. Foods prepared and cooked this way retain their natural textures and tastes. Another reason for careful cutting is to enhance the visual appeal of a dish. This is why most Chinese and Southeast Asian cuisines are so specific about cutting techniques, particularly where vegetables are concerned. The Chinese always use a cleaver (page 38) for these tasks, wielding it with skill and dexterity, but a sharp heavy knife can be used instead.

Chinese cooking is a sophisticated cuisine which involves a number of cooking methods which are relatively uncommon in the West; many of them have been adopted in other Asian cuisines. Sometimes several different cooking techniques are used in the preparation of a single dish, such as deep-frying bean curd and then braising it. Most of these techniques can be easily mastered with a little practice. When you are planning a meal, be sure to select dishes which use a range of techniques; limit yourself to one stir-fried dish per meal until you have become used to this important method of cooking.

▣ CUTTING TECHNIQUES

Slicing

This is the conventional method of slicing food. Hold the food firmly on the chopping board with one hand and slice the food straight down into very thin slices. If you use a cleaver rather than a knife for this, hold the cleaver with your index finger over the far side of the top of the cleaver and your thumb on the side nearest you to guide the cutting edge firmly. Hold the food with your other hand, turning your fingers under for safety. Your knuckles should act as a guide for the blade.

Horizontal or flat slicing

There is a technique for splitting food into 2 thinner pieces while retaining its overall shape. It can be used for cutting bean curd in half, for example. The cleaver, with its wide blade, is particularly suitable for this. Hold the blade of the cleaver or knife parallel to the chopping board, and place your free hand on top of the piece of food to keep it steady. Using a gentle cutting motion, slice horizontally through the food.

Diagonal slicing

This technique is used for cutting vegetables such as asparagus, carrots, or scallions. The purpose is to expose more of the surface of the vegetable for quicker cooking. Angle the knife or cleaver at a slant and cut.

Roll cutting

This is rather like diagonal slicing but is used for larger vegetables such as zucchini, large carrots, eggplant, and Chinese white radish. As with diagonal slicing, this technique allows more of the surface of the vegetable to be exposed to the heat, thereby speeding up the cooking time. Begin by making one diagonal slice at one end of the vegetable. Then turn it 180 degrees and make the next diagonal slice. Continue in this way until you have chopped the entire vegetable into evenly sized, diamond-shaped chunks.

Shredding

This is the process by which food is cut into thin, fine, matchsticklike shreds. First cut the food into slices, then pile several slices on top of each other and cut them *lengthways* into fine strips.

Dicing

This is a simple technique of cutting food into small cubes or dice. The food should first be cut into slices. Stack the slices and cut them again *lengthways* into sticks just as you would for shredding (above). Stack the strips or sticks and cut *crossways* into evenly sized cubes or dice.

Scoring

This is a technique used to pierce the surface of foods to help them cook faster and more evenly. It also gives them an attractive appearance. Use a cleaver or sharp knife and make cuts into the food at a slight angle to a depth of about ⅛ inch. Take care not to cut all the way through. Make cuts all over the surface of the food, cutting crisscross to give a wide, diamond-shaped pattern.

⊡ COOKING TECHNIQUES

Blanching

This involves putting food into hot water or into moderately hot oil for a few minutes to cook it briefly but not entirely. It is a sort of softening-up process to prepare the food for final cooking. Blanching in water is common with harder vegetables such as broccoli or carrots. The vegetable is plunged into boiling water for several minutes. It is then drained and plunged into cold water to arrest the cooking process. In such cases, blanching usually precedes stir-frying which completes the cooking.

Poaching

This is a method of simmering a food until it is partially cooked. It is then put into soup or combined with a sauce and the cooking process continued.

Stir-frying

This is the most famous of all Chinese cooking techniques and is used extensively. It is possibly the most tricky technique since success with it depends upon having all the required ingredients prepared, measured out, and immediately at hand, and on having a good source of fierce heat. Its advantage is that, properly executed, stir-fried foods can be cooked in minutes in very little oil so they retain their natural flavors and textures. It is very important that stir-fried foods not be overcooked or greasy. Once you have mastered this technique, you will find that it becomes almost second nature. Using a wok is definitely an advantage when stir-frying as its shape not only conducts the heat well, but its high sides enable you to toss and stir ingredients rapidly, keeping them constantly moving while cooking. Having prepared all the ingredients for stir-frying, follow the steps below.

- Heat the wok or frying-pan until it is very hot *before* adding the oil. This prevents food sticking and will ensure an even heat. Add the oil and using a metal spatula or long-handled spoon, distribute it evenly over the surface. It should be very hot indeed—almost smoking— before you add the next ingredient unless you are going on to flavor the oil.
- If you are flavoring the oil with garlic, scallions, ginger, dried red chilies or other seasoning, do not wait for the oil to get so hot that it is almost smoking. If you do, these ingredients will burn and become bitter. Toss them quickly in the oil for a few seconds. In some recipes, these flavorings will then be removed and discarded before cooking proceeds.

- Now add the ingredients as described in the recipe and proceed to stir-fry by tossing them over the surface of the wok or pan with the metal spatula or long-handled spoon. Keep moving the food from the center of the wok to the sides. Stir-frying is a noisy business and is usually accompanied by quite a lot of splattering because of the high temperature at which the food must be cooked.
- Some stir-fried dishes are thickened with a mixture of cornstarch and cold water. To avoid getting a lumpy sauce, be sure to remove the wok or pan from the heat before you add the cornstarch mixture, which must be thoroughly blended before it is added. The sauce can then be returned to the heat and thickened.

Deep-frying

This is one of the most important techniques in Asian cooking. The trick is to regulate the heat so that the surface of the food is sealed but does not brown so fast that the food is uncooked inside. Although deep-fried food must not be greasy, the process does require a lot of oil. The Chinese use a wok for deep-frying which requires less oil than a deep-fat fryer; however, I think you should avoid using a wok until you are very sure of it. When you do, be certain that it is fully secure on its stand before adding the oil or, if it is flat-bottomed, that it is secured on its own. On no account leave the wok unsupervised. Most people will find a deep-fat fryer easier and safer to use. Be careful not to fill this more than half-full with oil. Below are some points to bear in mind when deep-frying.

- Wait for the oil to get hot enough before adding the food to be fried. The oil should give off a haze and almost produce little wisps of smoke when it is the right temperature, but you can test it by dropping in a small piece of food. If it bubbles all over, then the oil is sufficiently hot. Adjust the heat as necessary to prevent the oil from actually smoking or overheating.

- Be sure to dry food to be deep-fried thoroughly first with kitchen paper as this will prevent splattering. If the food is in a marinade, remove it with a slotted spoon and drain before putting it into the oil. If you are using batter, make sure all the excess batter drips off before adding the food to the hot oil.
- Oil used for deep-frying can be re-used. Cool it and then strain into a jar through several layers of cheesecloth or through a fine mesh to remove any particles of food which might otherwise burn if reheated and give the oil a bitter taste. Label the jar according to what food you have cooked in the oil, and only re-use it for the same purpose. Oil can be used up to three times before it begins to lose its effectiveness.

Shallow-frying or pan-frying

This technique is similar to sautéeing. It involves more oil than stir-frying but less than for deep-frying. Food is fried first on one side and then on the other. Sometimes the excess oil is drained off and a sauce added to complete the dish. A frying-pan or a flat-bottomed wok is ideal for shallow-frying.

Slow-simmering and steeping

These processes are very similar. In slow-simmering, food is immersed in liquid which is brought almost to the boil and then the temperature is reduced so that it simmers, cooking the food to the desired degree. This is the technique used for making stock. In steeping, food is similarly immersed in liquid (usually stock) and simmered for a time. The heat is then turned off and the residual heat of the liquid finishes off the cooking process.

Braising and red-braising

These techniques are most often applied to certain vegetables. The food is usually browned or deep-fried and then put into stock which has been flavored with seasonings and spices. The stock is brought to the boil, the heat reduced and the food simmered gently until it is cooked. Red-braising, which is also known as red-cooking, is simply the technique by which food is braised in a dark liquid such as soy sauce. This gives food a reddish brown color, hence the name. This type of braising sauce can be saved and frozen for re-use. It can be reused many times and becomes richer in flavor.

Steaming

Steaming has been used by the Chinese for thousands of years. Along with stir-frying and deep-frying, it is the most widely used technique. Steamed foods are cooked by a gentle moist heat which must circulate freely in order to cook the food. It is an excellent method for bringing out subtle flavors and so is particularly good for fish. Vegetables are almost never steamed; they are blanched instead. Bamboo steamers are used by the Chinese, but you could choose from a variety of utensils.

Using a bamboo steamer in a wok For this you need a large bamboo steamer about 10-inches wide. Put about 2-inches of water in a wok and bring to a simmer. Put the bamboo steamer containing the food into the wok where it should rest safely perched on the sloping sides. Cover the steamer with its matching lid and steam the food until it is cooked. Replenish the water as required.

Using a wok as a steamer Put about 2-inches of water into a wok and then place a metal or wooden rack into the wok. Bring the water to a simmer and put the food to be steamed onto a heatproof plate. Lower the plate onto the rack and cover the wok tightly with the lid. Check the water level from time to time and replenish it with hot water when necessary.

Using a large roasting pan or pot as a steamer Put a metal or wooden rack into the pan or pot and pour in about 2-inches of water. Bring to a simmer and put the food to be steamed onto a heatproof plate. Lower the plate onto the rack and cover the pan or pot with a lid or with aluminum foil. Replenish the water as necessary.

If you do not have a metal or wooden rack, you could use a small empty can to support the plate of food. Remember that the food needs to remain above the water level and must not get wet. The water level should always be at least 1 inch below the edge of the plate. (Be sure to use a heatproof plate.)

Using a European steamer   If you have a metal steamer which is wide enough to take a plate of food, then this will give you very satisfactory results. Keep an eye on the level of the water in the base.

Reheating foods

Steaming is one of the best methods of reheating food since it warms the food without cooking it further and without drying it out. To reheat soups and braised dishes, bring the liquid slowly to a simmer but do not boil. Remove it from the heat as soon as it is hot to prevent overcooking.

Thickening

Cornstarch blended with an equal quantity of water is frequently used in Chinese cookery to thicken sauces and glaze dishes. Always make sure the mixture is smooth and well blended before adding it.

Starters & Appetizers

Starters and appetizers are meant to stimulate the palate, to prepare one for the offerings to come. As such, I like them to be subtly appealing in taste and textures. In most cases, they should be simple and light for you don't wish to overwhelm the main course. And yet some appetizers, like Northern Chinese Vegetable Potstickers, are almost a meal in themselves. Indeed, it is not uncommon when dining out in an Asian restaurant to see people make their selections only from the appetizer section of the menu. The rule here is to make and use the recipes as they fit into your meal or menu. They may be used as starters; as a first course in a series of courses; or as a part of many courses—that is, if you wish to follow the Asian custom of including many courses on the table at once; or you may serve them as another dish in a family meal. Use these appetizers with all styles of cookery, not just Asian. Be imaginative and combine or match these appetizers with other foods and beverages, or serve them as mini-meals in themselves.

Thai corn pancakes

2 pounds fresh corn on the
   cob, or 2½ cups canned
   corn
2 eggs, beaten
1 tablespoon cornstarch
2 tablespoons finely chopped
   fresh coriander
1 tablespoon finely chopped
   garlic
2 teapoons finely chopped
   fresh ginger
¼ teaspoon black pepper
1 teaspoon salt
2 tablespoons coarsely
   chopped fresh chilies
1 tablespoon peanut oil

 Serves 4 to 6

Corn is one of the numerous "New World" vegetables—along with tomatoes, white and sweet potatoes, peppers, and chilies—introduced relatively recently into Asia and now extremely popular ingredients in these cuisines. Thai cooking often uses corn in its dishes and these hot and spicy pancakes are typical of Thai food. I prefer it even hotter, but if you wish you may cut down on the chilies. Delicious served warm or cold, these pancakes make an excellent starter but may also be served as a side vegetable dish to a main course. ▪

Remove the corn kernels from the cob with a sharp knife or cleaver. You should end up with about 2½ cups. If you are using canned corn, empty the contents and drain thoroughly. Set aside half of the corn in a separate bowl, combine the rest of the corn with the rest of the ingredient except the oil, and purée it in a blender. Fold in the remaining corn.

    Heat a frying-pan, preferably non-stick, add the oil, and spoon in 2 tablespoons of the mixture. Cook the pancake over medium heat for 2 to 3 minutes or until brown on one side. Using a knife or spatula, turn the pancake over and cook the other side until crisp and golden. Continue until you have used up all the mixture.

CHINESE PANCAKES

1¼ cups all-purpose flour
1 cup very hot water
2 tablespoons sesame oil

 Serves 6 to 8

These are simply flour-and-water pancakes with no seasonings or spices. As such, they blend perfectly with a variety of dishes, such as Mu-shu Vegetables (page 116), and serve as the basis of other dishes, such as Scallion Pancakes (page 53). They are used like bread in the West. Once you have the knack—practice, practice—they are easy to make. The unusual method of rolling "double" pancakes is designed to ensure thinner, moister pancakes with less chance of being overcooked. Because they can be frozen, it is possible to make a batch many days, even weeks, ahead of time. Thaw thoroughly before steaming them. These pancakes can be used with practically any stir-fried dish which does not contain too much sauce. ▪

Put the flour into a large bowl. Stir the hot water gradually into the flour, mixing continuously with chopsticks or a fork until the water is fully incorporated. Add more water if the mixture seems dry. Remove the mixture from the bowl and knead it with your hands. Return it to the bowl, cover with a clean, damp towel and let it rest for about 30 minutes.

After the resting period, take the dough out of the bowl and knead again for about 5 minutes, dusting with a little flour if sticky. Once the dough is smooth, form it into a roll about 18 inches long and about 1 inch in diameter. Take a knife and cut the roll into equal segments. There should be about 18. Roll each segment into a ball.

Take 2 of the dough balls. Dip one side of one ball into the sesame oil and place the oiled side on top of the other ball. Use a rolling pin and roll the 2 pancakes simultaneously into a circle about 6 inches in diameter. It is important to roll double pancakes in this way because the resulting dough will remain moist inside and you will be able to roll them thinner, but avoid the risk of overcooking them later. Place a frying-pan or wok over a very low heat. Put the double pancake into the pan and cook until dried on one side. Flip the pancakes over and cook the other side. Remove from the pan, peel the 2 pancakes apart and set aside. Repeat this process until all the dough balls have been cooked.

Steam the pancakes to reheat them, or alternatively, you could wrap them tightly in a double sheet of foil and put them into a pan containing 1 inch boiling water. Cover the pan, turn the heat down very low, and simmer until they are reheated. Don't be tempted to reheat the pancakes in the oven as this will dry them out too much. If you want to freeze the cooked pancakes, wrap them tightly in freezerwrap. When using pancakes which have been frozen, let them thaw in the refrigerator first before reheating.

Scallion pancakes

Pancake dough (page 51)
8 scallions, finely chopped
1 tablespoon salt
1 tablespoon sesame oil
2 to 3 tablespoons peanut oil

 Makes about 8 pancakes

Pancakes are familiar items in practically every cuisine. This particular type is popular in northern China, where winters are cold and harsh. They are slightly doughy and heavy but are nonetheless delicious and especially appropriate on cold winter days. In China, they are eaten with noodle soup or rice gruel in the mornings. Western habits and palates find them more suitable as starters or snacks with drinks. Pan-fried in oil with scallions and sesame oil, these pancakes have an enticing, pungent aroma that gives the appetite an edge. They should be consumed while still warm. Although I like to use them as a starter, they are equally good as a snack with a bowl of hot soup or noodles. Use a non-stick pan and experiment with using as little oil as possible. The authentic original version is slightly too oily for my taste. ■

Make up the pancake dough according to the recipe for Chinese Pancakes (page 51). After the resting period, take the dough out of the bowl and knead it again for about 5 minutes, dusting with a little flour if sticky. Add the scallions, salt, and sesame oil, and knead the dough well.

Divide the dough into 8 equal pieces. Roll each piece into a circle about 6 inches in diameter.

Place a non-stick frying-pan or wok over low heat. Add enough oil to lightly coat the bottom of the pan. Put the pancakes into the pan, making sure the edges do not touch, and cook until the pancakes are crispy on one side. Flip them over and cook on the other side. You may have to do this in several batches. Cut them into wedges and serve at once.

Sugar walnuts

½ cup walnuts, shelled
1¼ cups peanut oil, for deep-
frying
Syrup
2 cups water
4 tablespoons sugar
2 star anise
1 cinnamon stick or Chinese
cinnamon bark
3 tablespoons honey

 Serves 2 to 4

Walnuts, native to Asia, Europe, and North America, hardly need an introduction. As might be expected, there are many ways of using them in various cuisines of the world. Here, I have added the distinctive flavors of anise and cinnamon—walnuts are hearty enough to handle them, even though the blanching process has moderated the walnuts' slight bitterness. Cooking them in the syrup and allowing them to dry gives the walnut a tasty coating and seals in the syrup flavors. Delicious served as an appetizer with drinks, these walnuts are also used in the recipe Crispy Cabbage with Sugar Walnuts (page 64), forming a classic combination of sweet and salty tastes, and crunchy and delicate crispness.

Once deep-fried, the walnuts can be stored in a tightly covered glass jar for at least one week. The recipe can easily be doubled. ▪

Preheat the oven to its lowest temperature, then switch off.

Bring a saucepan of water to boil. Add the walnuts and cook for 2 minutes to blanch. Drain the nuts in a colander or sieve. Mix the syrup ingredients together in a pan. Combine the nuts with the syrup mixture and boil for 10 minutes or until the syrup mixture thickens. Remove the nuts with a slotted spoon, place on a baking pan and dry in the oven for at least 2 hours.

Heat the oil in a deep-fat fryer or wok to a moderate heat. Fry a batch of walnuts for about 2 minutes or until the walnuts turn dark brown (watch the heat to prevent burning). Remove the walnuts with a slotted spoon or strainer and lay them on a baking pan to cool. Deep-fry and drain the rest of the walnuts in the same way. Serve them warm with the Crispy Cabbage or cold with drinks.

Vietnamese-style Vegetarian Spring Rolls

1 package rice paper
    wrappers
2 cups peanut oil, for deep-
    frying

STUFFING

2 ounces bean thread
    (transparent) noodles
¼ cup carrots, finely
    shredded
½ cup snow peas, finely
    shredded
3 tablespoons scallions, finely
    chopped
1 teaspoon sesame oil
2 tablespoons light soy sauce
1 teaspoon Chinese rice wine
    or dry sherry

TO SERVE

1 cup iceberg lettuce
Assorted sprigs of basil, mint,
    or coriander, or a
    combination of all three
Spicy peanut sauce (page 57)

 Makes about 25 small spring rolls

Spring rolls are very much a Chinese dish but, to my taste, the Vietnamese version is the best. They are made with rice paper wrappers instead of a flour pancake, and this renders them lighter and crisper. I like the traditional practice of wrapping the cooked spring rolls in a fresh lettuce leaf with mint, basil, or fresh coriander leaves and dipping them in a spicy peanut sauce. Such spring rolls are a splendid opener to any meal. The rice paper wrappers can be found in Asian specialty markets. They are dry and must be gently soaked before using them. Handle them with care as they are quite fragile. When deep-frying the spring rolls, do not crowd them in the pan as they tend to stick. ■

For the stuffing, soak the noodles in a large bowl of warm water for 15 minutes. When they are soft, drain them and discard the water. Cut the noodles into 3-inch lengths, using scissors or a knife.

In a large bowl, mix the noodles with the carrots, snow peas, scallions, sesame oil, light soy sauce, and rice wine.

To make the spring rolls, fill a large bowl with warm water and

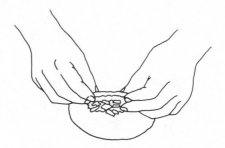

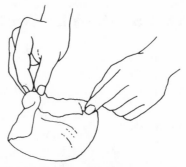

dip one of the rice paper wrappers in the water to soften. Remove and drain on a linen towel. Put about 2 tablespoons of the filling on each softened rice paper wrapper. Fold in each side and then roll up tightly.

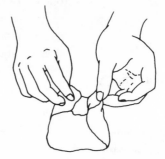

They will seal by themselves. You should have a roll about 3 inches long, a little like a small sausage. Repeat the procedure until you have used up all the filling.

Heat the oil in a deep-fat fryer or a large wok until it is hot. Deep-fry the spring rolls, a few at a time, until golden brown, about 2 minutes. They have a tendency to stick to each other at the beginning of the frying, so only fry a few at a time. Drain them on paper towel. Serve at once with lettuce leaves, herb sprigs, and dipping sauce (page 19).

Spicy peanut sauce

1 tablespoon fish sauce
2 tablespoons Chinese white rice vinegar or cider vinegar
½ teaspoon finely chopped garlic
3 tablespoons roasted peanuts, coarsely chopped
1 teaspoon chili oil
2 tablespoons water
1 teaspoon sugar

 Makes enough for about 25 small spring rolls

Dipping sauces are common in all far Eastern cuisines. Here is a tasty Southeast Asian version, commonly used with spring rolls. It has a peanut flavor but the secret charm of this dip lies in the addition of fish sauce, an essential ingredient which you should try to obtain. You may adjust the chili oil to suit your own palate. This sauce may be made well ahead of time. ▪

Combine all the ingredients together in a small bowl, mixing thoroughly. Let the dipping sauce stand at least 10 minutes before using.

Northern chinese vegetable potstickers

1 package potsticker
  wrappers, bought or made
  according to the recipe
  below

DOUGH
²/₃ cup all purpose flour
½ cup very hot water

STUFFING
½ cup fresh or frozen peas
¼ cup finely chopped
  Sichuan preserved
  vegetables
2 tablespoons finely chopped
  garlic
1 cup finely chopped bok
  choy
1 cup coarsely chopped
  Chinese chives
¼ teaspoon salt
pinch freshly ground pepper
2 tablespoons rice wine or
  dry sherry
1 tablespoon dark soy sauce
2 teaspoons sugar
3 tablespoons peanut oil
²/₃ cup water

 Makes about 20 dumplings

Potstickers are a form of dumpling and, in northern China, they are a specialty in restaurants and a staple in home kitchens. To this day, making them is a family affair and social occasion, with Sunday mornings before the big lunch meal devoted to their preparation. In general, dumplings may be shallow-fried, boiled, poached, or steamed. One very popular way to make them is to shallow-fry in oil and water until they literally stick to the pan, a method I like best of all. Properly done, it produces true potsticker dumplings that are crisp on the bottom, soft on the top, and juicy inside. The goal is to have a contrast of textures and flavors.

In China, potsticker dumplings usually include minced pork. Here, I omit the pork and offer a vegetarian one that is completely satisfying. Try to obtain the Chinese preserved vegetables and Chinese chives; they add an excellent flavor to the dumplings. You may substitute regular chives, but there is really no substitute for the preserved vegetables. Make your own dipping sauce with chili oil, dark soy sauce, and Chinese white rice vinegar or cider vinegar.

Potsticker dumplings may be frozen uncooked and can be transferred directly from the freezer to the pan; just cook them a little longer than usual. Ready-made potsticker wrappers can be found in many supermarkets or Asian specialty markets if you choose not to make your own. ∎

If you are making the dough, put the flour into a large bowl and gradually stir in the hot water, mixing continuously with a fork or chopsticks until most of the water is incorporated. Add more water if the mixture seems dry. Remove the dough from the bowl and knead it with your hands until smooth. This should take about 5 minutes. Put the dough back into the bowl, cover it with a clean, damp, towel and let it rest for about 20 minutes.

While the dough is resting, make the stuffing. If you are using fresh peas, blanch them in a pan of boiling water for 4 minutes or 2 minutes if they are frozen. Rinse the Sichuan preserved vegetables several times in cold water and blot them dry.

Heat a wok or large frying-pan over high heat and add 1 tablespoon of oil. Add the stuffing ingredients and stir-fry for 5 minutes or until the mixture is dry. Remove the mixture to a bowl and allow the stuffing ingredients to cool thoroughly.

After the resting time, take the dough out of the bowl and knead it again for about 5 minutes, dusting it with a little flour if sticky. Once the dough is smooth, form it into a roll about 9 inches long and about 1 inch in diameter. Take a knife and cut the roll into 18 equal pieces.

Roll each piece of dough into a small ball, then roll each ball into a small, round, flat "pancake" about 2½ inches in diameter. Arrange the rounds on a lightly floured tray and cover with a damp kitchen towel to keep them from drying out until required.

Put about 1 tablespoon of filling in the center of each pancake, then fold in half. Moisten the edges with water and pinch together

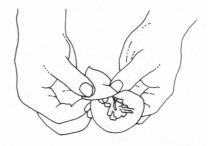

with your fingers. Pleat around the edge, pinching to seal well. Transfer the finished dumplings to the floured tray and keep it covered with a damp cloth until you have filled all the dumplings in this way.

Heat a frying-pan (preferably non-stick) over a high heat until hot and add 1 tablespoon of oil. Place the dumplings, flat side down, into the pan. Turn down the heat and cook for 2 minutes until lightly browned. (You may need to cook the dumplings in two batches.) Add the ⅔ cup water, cover the pan tightly, and cook for about 12 minutes or until most of the liquid is absorbed. Uncover the pan and continue to cook for 2 minutes longer. Remove the dumplings and serve.

Place three bowls on the table, containing Chinese white rice vinegar, chili oil, and dark soy sauce. Let each person concoct their own dipping sauce by mixing these three items exactly to their taste.

Hot and spicy walnuts

½ pound walnuts, shelled
2 tablespoons chili bean
    sauce
1 tablespoon finely chopped
    garlic
1 tablespoon finely chopped
    fresh ginger
3 tablespoons Chinese black
    rice vinegar or cider
    vinegar
2 tablespoons sugar
2 tablespoons dark soy sauce
2 tablespoons Chinese white
    rice vinegar or cider
    vinegar
2⅔ cups water
2 cups peanut oil, for deep-
    frying

GARNISH

3 tablespoons finely chopped
    scallions

 *Serves 4 to 6*

This is a spicy, savory way to prepare walnuts to be served either as a snack with drinks or as a crunchy addition to other stir-fry dishes. Prepared in this way, the walnuts lend themselves to many uses; use your imagination and experiment with them. You may want to try them with Crispy Cabbage (page 64) instead of using the sugar walnuts. If the walnuts get soft before they are used, you may recrisp them by heating them in a warm oven. They can be made ahead of time but should be eaten within a few days of their preparation. They do not keep for a long time because of the seasonings used in this recipe. ▪

Bring a saucepan of water to the boil. Add the walnuts and simmer for about 5 minutes to blanch. Drain the nuts in a colander or sieve, then pat dry with paper towel.

Combine all the remaining ingredients together in a saucepan. Add the walnuts and cook for about 20 minutes over high heat. Drain the nuts and spread them on a baking pan to dry. Let them dry for at least 2 hours or more.

Heat the oil in a deep-fat fryer or wok to a moderate heat. Fry some of the walnuts for about 3 minutes or until they turn deep brown and crispy. (Watch the heat to prevent burning.) You may have to deep-fry them in several batches. Remove the walnuts with a slotted spoon or strainer. Drain on paper towel. Allow them to cool and become crisp before serving. Garnish them with the scallions.

CRISPY VEGETARIAN WONTONS

1 package wonton skins
   (about 30–35)
2 cups peanut oil, for deep-
   frying
Hoisin sauce, for dipping

FILLING

1 tablespoon peanut oil
¼ cup carrots, finely
   shredded
½ cup cabbage, finely
   shredded
¼ cup bean sprouts
2 tablespoons finely chopped
   garlic
1 tablespoon dark soy sauce
3 tablespoons mashed bean
   curd
1 teaspoon sugar
½ teaspoon salt
1 teaspoon sesame oil
½ teaspoon freshly ground
   black pepper

Makes 30–35 wontons

Wontons stuffed with tasty fillings of flavorful meat or vegetables are universally appreciated. This is a vegetarian version of the traditional Chinese treat with a filling of carrots, cabbage, bean sprouts, and with bean curd for body. These wontons are delicious with hoisin sauce or, if you prefer, a dipping sauce made with your own combination of chili oil, white rice wine vinegar, and light soy sauce. These wontons are ideal with drinks or as a starter.

Do *not* make them too far ahead of time. Because they are made with a moisture-laden vegetable stuffing, the wonton skins will soften in an unpalatable way if they are allowed to sit for a long time. If possible, make and serve them straight away. ■

For the filling, heat a wok or large frying-pan and add the oil. When moderately hot, add the carrots, cabbage, bean sprouts, and garlic and stir-fry for 1 minute. Set aside to cool thoroughly.

Combine the cooled vegetables with the rest of the filling ingredients and mix well. Using a teaspoon, put a small amount of filling

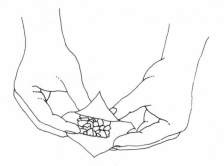

in the center of each wonton skin. Bring up 2 opposite corners, dampen the edges with a little water, and pinch them together to make a triangle. Fold over the bottom 2 corners so they overlap, and press together. The filling should be well sealed in.

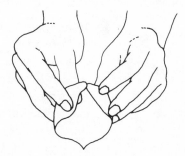

Heat the oil in a deep-fat fryer or large wok until hot. Deep-fry the filled wontons in several batches. Drain on paper towel. Serve at once with hoisin sauce.

CRISPY CABBAGE WITH SUGAR WALNUTS

¾ cup canned red-in-snow
  cabbage
1¼ cups peanut oil for deep-
  frying
Sugar Walnuts (page 54)

 Serves 4

In northern China, I understand, there is a true seaweed dish, but in my experience, what is called "seaweed" here, is most likely fresh Chinese greens shredded and dried. The taste is fine but I prefer this version from The Sichuan Garden restaurant in Hong Kong. It uses a canned preserved cabbage called red-in-snow which is a pickled vegetable, traditional among the people of Chekiang and Kiangsu in northern China. It looks like turnip tops, and both leaves and stalks are preserved. In the late winter or early spring, the red roots of the plant are often visible through the snow, hence its name. If you cannot find it, use Chinese cabbage, finely shredded and thoroughly dried in the oven. The key to the success of this dish is to be sure the red-in-snow cabbage is thoroughly dried and the oil quite hot. Serve the dish at once. ■

Rinse the cabbage in several changes of cold water. Place on a linen towel and squeeze out all the excess liquid.

Heat the oil in a deep-fat fryer or wok until it almost smokes. Deep-fry half of the cabbage for about 3 minutes or until crispy, and then drain on paper towel. Repeat the process with the remaining cabbage.

Mix the walnuts with the cabbage and serve at once.

Eggplant with sesame sauce

1½ pounds Chinese eggplants
or ordinary eggplant

SAUCE

1 tablespoon sesame paste
½ teaspoon roasted Sichuan
  peppercorns (page 30)
2 tablespoons sesame oil
2 teaspoons chili oil
2 teaspoons sugar
1 teaspoon Chinese white rice
  vinegar or cider vinegar
½ teaspoon finely chopped
  garlic
½ teaspoon finely chopped
  fresh ginger
2 tablespoons finely chopped
  scallions
1 tablespoon dark soy sauce

 Serves 4, as a starter

This is a very easy and delicious way to prepare eggplant. Try to obtain the smaller, more delicately flavored Chinese eggplants if you can. The cooking process produces sweet, tender, and moist eggplant meat, and increases its receptivity to the classic Sichuan sauce: garlic, ginger, and scallions. This dish makes a delicious appetizer and, as it is served cold, may be made hours in advance. The sauce, however, should not be poured over the cooked eggplant until just before serving. ■

Preheat the oven to 400°F. Put the eggplants in a roasting pan and bake about 30 minutes if they are the Chinese variety, or 45 minutes if they are the larger variety. They should be charred outside and tender inside. Allow them to cool thoroughly.

Peel the eggplants and shred the flesh or cut into strips. Arrange the eggplants on a serving plate.

Mix all the sauce ingredients together in a small bowl. Just before serving, pour this over the eggplants.

Spicy korean kimchi

1 pound Chinese cabbage
2 tablespoons salt
4 cups cold water
2 cups very hot water

PICKLING MIXTURE

1 tablespoon finely chopped
    garlic
1 tablespoon finely chopped
    fresh ginger
1 tablespoon finely chopped
    scallions
2 teaspoons finely chopped
    dried chili
2 teaspoons sugar
1 tablespoon salt

 Makes about 1 pound

Pickled vegetables are a specialty in Asian cuisines. This is understandable, given the abundance of vegetables on the one hand and the absence of refrigeration (until quite recently) on the other. Necessity generated inventiveness and imagination to preserve the foods in a palatable way. Korean meals almost always include a pickled vegetable, "kimchi," as it is called generically, to stimulate the palate and as a contrast to less fiery foods. In the West, we use our pickled dishes more sparingly, serving them on picnics or with cold platters. In this adaptation of Korean "kimchi," I follow the traditional method of fermentation without the use of vinegar. The leaves develop a slightly sour taste enlivened by chili—if you find it too "hot," reduce the chili. Pickled cabbage is sold in glass jars in Asian specialty markets, but it is usually full of preservatives and monosodium glutamates. I urge you to make your own; it is quite simple, can be prepared in advance, and keeps for weeks in the refrigerator. ■

Separate the leaves and sprinkle them with the salt. Pour in the cold water and allow them to stand in a cool place for 8 hours or overnight. Rinse the cabbage well and squeeze out the excess liquid.

Boil the water and pour over the pickling mixture. Mix well and combine with the cabbage leaves. Put the leaves with the pickling mixture into a large glass bowl. You may have to cut the leaves in half to make them fit. Cover the kimchi with plastic wrap and leave in a cool place for about 2 days. Drain and cut the leaves into bite-size pieces. Pack into a glass jar until ready to serve.

Winter vegetable fritters

¼ pound carrots
¼ pound fresh or canned
   water chestnuts
¼ pound cabbage
1 small onion
6 tablespoons all-purpose
   flour
1 tablespoon cornstarch
3 eggs, beaten
2 teaspoons salt
2 teaspoons baking powder
2 teaspoons sugar
1 teaspoon freshly ground
   black pepper
3 to 4 tablespoons peanut oil

 *Serves 2 to 4*

These vegetable fritters (similar to pancakes), served warm or at room temperature, are an appetising starter for any meal. You may substitute other vegetables as long as they are firm, such as cucumbers or zucchini. The key ingredient in this version is fresh water chestnuts—try to obtain them, for they add a special sweetness and texture to the fritters. Served with a simple green salad, these vegetable fritters also make a delicious light luncheon. ▪

Finely chop the carrots, water chestnuts, cabbage, and onion. Lightly blend all the ingredients, except the oil, in a food processor or a food mill for a few seconds. Do not use a blender.

Heat a frying-pan or a wok and add the oil. Spoon in 3 tablespoons of the mixture to make a 4-inch wide pancake and fry for 2 to 3 minutes or until golden brown on one side. Using a knife or spatula, turn the pancake over and cook the other side until crispy and golden. Continue this process until you have used up all the mixture. Cut the fritters into wedges and serve.

JAPANESE-STYLE MARINATED MUSHROOMS

1 pound small button
mushrooms

MARINADE

⅔ cup sake, rice wine, or dry
sherry
2 tablespoons light soy sauce
2 teaspoons sugar
1 tablespoon Chinese white
rice vinegar or cider
vinegar
½ teaspoon salt

GARNISH

2 tablespoons finely chopped
scallions

 Serves 4

What could be easier than a dish that requires no cooking? Well, almost no cooking: the marinade must be heated and it in turn "cooks" the mushrooms overnight. This simple and delicious appetizer also makes a splendid side dish for roasted meats. ■

Place the marinade ingredients in a small pan and simmer for about 5 minutes. Allow to cool thoroughly. Combine the cooled marinade with the whole mushrooms and let them marinade overnight.

When ready to serve the mushrooms, drain them and discard the marinade.

CRUNCHY RADISH SALAD

¾ pound Chinese white
   radish
2 teaspoons salt

DRESSING

¼ teaspoon roasted Sichuan
   peppercorns (page 30)
1 tablespoon light soy sauce
1 teaspoon sugar
1 tablespoon sesame oil

Serves 2 to 4

Looking like long, overgrown white carrots, these radishes are a staple in Chinese cookery. I have seen them referred to as "Icicle Radish," "Chinese Turnip" and "Rettish." In China, they are never eaten raw, but I enjoy their crunchy texture, especially in salads such as this. They have a mild peppery taste which is muted by cooking them; in this recipe, they are salted to remove the bite. Once this is done, the radishes lend themselves very well to other spices and seasonings, as in this Chinese dressing of soy sauce, sugar, pepper, and sesame oil. Remember that the cool, crunchy bite of Chinese radishes works well with Western-type dressings, so do experiment. If you cannot obtain the Chinese version, substitute ordinary radishes but cut them in half to show off their whiteness and expose them to the dressing. (Salting ordinary radishes is optional.) ■

Cut the radish into 3-inch long by ¼-inch thick pieces. Salt the pieces, toss to mix thoroughly, and set aside for 20 minutes. Rinse the radish and pat them dry with paper towel.

    For the dressing, first roast the peppercorns. Combine all the dressing ingredients and pour over the radish. Mix thoroughly and serve.

Soups

Soup is excellent either to start a meal or as a meal in itself. In Asia, soups are often served as part of a meal, as one of the courses on the table; it also serves as a beverage. In this book, there are two types of soups: hearty and rich such as Fiery Sichuan Soup or Sizzling Rice Soup and light, brothy ones, such as Tangy Tomato Soup with Lemongrass or Steamed Vegetable Soup. They may be used either as part of an Asian-style menu or in your everyday meals. Many are simple and easy to put together, especially if you have the stock already prepared.

The key to *any* good soup is the stock. It is virtually impossible to have a good soup without it. Although it takes a little effort and work to make a good stock, the rewards make it well worthwhile. Many of the soups in this book are based on either chicken or vegetable stock depending upon your preference. The Japanese recipes use dashi, a fish-based stock (page 22), but chicken or vegetable can be substituted.

CHICKEN STOCK

Good stock is essential to all cuisines. This is especially true for a cuisine that relies upon vegetables and pasta. Because of its lightness, flavor, and versatility, chicken stock should be considered a staple like salt, cooking oil, or soy sauce. There are commercially prepared canned or cubed stocks, but many of them are inferior in quality, being too salty or containing additives and food dyes. Try to make your own, as the best chicken stock is homemade. Since I am not a vegetarian, I usually make up a large batch of it and freeze in smaller portions for future use. Remember,—*stock is the foundation of all good cooking*. Here are a few rules to remember when making chicken stock:

- It is best to use 50 percent bones and 50 percent meat. Without meat, the stock will not have the necessary body, richness, or depth. Stewing (old) hens are best, because they are inexpensive (if you can find them) and full of flavor.
- Stock should simmer. Never let the stock come to a boil because that will result in a cloudy and heavy stock. Good flavor and digestibility come with a clear stock.
- Use a deep heavy saucepan so the liquid covers all the solids and evaporation is slow.
- Simmer on low heat and gently skim the stock every now and then to remove any impurities.
- Strain the stock slowly through several layers of cheesecloth or a fine mesh strainer.
- Allow the stock to cool thoroughly before freezing.

6 pounds chicken pieces,
  bones (backs, feet, wings,
  etc.)
1¾ quarts cold water
4 slices fresh ginger
4 scallions
4 large garlic cloves
2 teaspoons Sichuan
  peppercorns, unroasted
2 teaspoons black
  peppercorns
½ teaspoon salt

If you make a habit of saving your uncooked chicken bones and carcasses, you will have the essential ingredient for stock in no time. It also makes good economic sense. ■

Put the chicken pieces and bones into a very large saucepan. (The bones can be put in either frozen or defrosted.) Cover with the cold water and bring it to a simmer.

Meanwhile cut the ginger into diagonal slices, 2-inches by 1¼-inch. Remove the green tops from the scallions. Lightly crush the garlic cloves leaving the skins on.

Using a large, flat spoon, gently skim off the scum as it rises from the bones. Watch the heat as the stock should *never* boil. Keep skimming until the stock looks clear. This can take from 20 to 40 minutes. Do not stir or disturb the stock.

Reduce the heat to a gentle simmer. Add the ginger, white parts of the scallions, garlic, peppercorns, and salt. Simmer the stock over a very low heat for between 2 to 4 hours, skimming any fat off the top at least twice during this time. The stock should be rich and full-bodied, which is why it needs to be simmered for such a long time. This way the stock (and any soup you make with it) will have plenty of flavor.

Strain the stock through several layers of dampened cheesecloth or through a very fine mesh strainer. Let it cool thoroughly. Remove any fat which has risen to the top. It is now ready to be used or transferred to containers and frozen for future use.

VEGETABLE STOCK

1 ounce Chinese dried
   mushrooms
2 pounds carrots
4 celery sticks
2 pounds onions
4 leeks
½ pound shallots
2 tablespoons peanut oil
6 scallions
6 slices fresh ginger
8 garlic cloves, peeled and
   crushed
1 tablespoon black
   peppercorns
1 tablespoon Sichuan
   peppercorns, unroasted
4 bay leaves
2 tablespoons salt
4 quarts water
3 tablespoons light soy sauce

 Makes about 8 pints

I prefer chicken stock to any other, but I include this vegetable stock as an alternative. Vegetarian cooking presents a problem when it comes to stock. In the absence of poultry, fish, or meat, it is difficult to prepare a rich stock, the foundation of any cuisine. Vegetable stocks tend to be comparatively weak and lack robustness. Even in China, the custom has been to add the additive monosodium glutimate to vegetable stock. Another popular vegetable stock employs the peppery bite of white radish to impart body in it. With my colleague Gordon Wing, I have experimented and found that cooking the vegetables in oil *before* simmering helps to impart flavor to the stock. Gordon suggests using dried Chinese mushrooms to add richness and depth. If you find the portions too large for your needs, cut the recipe in half. ◾

If you are using the dried mushrooms, soak them in warm water for 20 minutes. Drain, squeeze out any excess liquid, and coarsely chop the mushrooms, caps and stems.

Coarsely chop the carrots, celery, and onions. Wash, cut, and discard the green part of the leeks, and coarsely chop the white portion. Peel the shallots but leave them whole.

Heat a large saucepan or wok over moderate heat and add the oil. Put in the scallions, ginger, garlic, and shallots, and stir-fry for 1 minute. Then add the carrots, celery, leeks, and onions and continue to cook for 5 minutes. Put all the vegetables and the rest of the ingredients into a very large pan. Cover them with the cold water and bring it to a simmer.

Using a large, flat spoon, skim off the foam as it rises to the top. This will take about 5 minutes. Bring the stock to a boil. Reduce the heat to moderate and simmer for about 2 hours.

Strain the stock through a large colander, then through a very fine mesh strainer. Let it cool thoroughly. It is now ready to be used or transferred to containers and frozen for future use.

Soft bean curd and spinach soup

2 ounces bean thread noodles
1½ pounds fresh spinach
8 ounces soft bean curd
1 quart chicken or vegetable stock
2 tablespoons light soy sauce
3 tablespoons rice wine or dry sherry
2 teaspoons sugar
½ teaspoon salt

 Serves 4

This simple but delicious and nutritious soup is one you would often find on the table in China. Use *soft* bean curd: its custard-like texture and mild flavor works with the sugar to neutralize the metallic edge of the spinach. The bean thread noodles give substance to this warming dish. ▪

Soak the noodles in a large bowl of warm water for 15 minutes. When soft, drain them and discard the water. Cut the noodles into 3-inch lengths using scissors or a knife. Remove the stalks from the spinach and wash the leaves well. Gently cut the bean curd into 1-inch cubes.

Put the stock into a saucepan and bring to a simmer. Add the bean thread noodles and simmer for 2 minutes. Add the spinach and the rest of the ingredients except the bean curd. Simmer for 2 minutes, then gently put in the bean curd. Continue to simmer the soup for 2 more minutes to heat the bean curd through and serve at once.

Tangy tomato soup with lemongrass

1 quart chicken or vegetable
stock
1 pound fresh or canned
tomatoes
1 fresh lemongrass stalk or 1
tablespoon finely chopped
lemon zest
1½ teaspoons salt
2 teaspoons sugar
1 tablespoon lemon juice
2 tablespoons finely chopped
scallions
1 small chili, sliced
1 tablespoon finely chopped
coriander
1 egg white
2 teaspoons sesame oil

GARNISH
coriander leaves

 Serves 2 to 4

This Thai-Chinese combination is so intimately intertwined that it is difficult to differentiate the various contributors. The Thai cuisine specializes in hot, tangy, spicy soups that are refreshing and stimulating. The Chinese cuisine includes many soups that are as beautiful as they are delicious. The eggflower motif—lovely strands of lace-like white of egg—is a common one and is here set within the colorful context of bright red tomatoes. The lemongrass, refreshing and aromatic, is used in both cuisines. This impressive yet easy to make soup could be served at the grandest dinner. Alternatively, simply add blanched rice noodles to the soup and it becomes a meal in itself. ■

Put the stock in a saucepan and bring it to a simmer. If using fresh tomatoes, peel, seed, and cut them into 1-inch cubes. If using canned tomatoes, chop them into small chunks. Peel the lemongrass stalk until you find the tender, whitish center and finely chop it.

Add the salt, sugar, lemon juice, scallions, chili, and coriander to the simmering stock and stir to mix well. Add the tomatoes and simmer for 3 minutes. Lightly beat the egg white and then combine it with the sesame oil in a small bowl. Pour the egg white mixture into the soup in a very slow, thin stream. Using a chopstick or fork, pull the egg slowly into strands. (I have found that stirring the egg white in a figure-eight works quite well.) Garnish with the coriander leaves and serve.

Sizzling rice soup

1 ounce Chinese dried
  mushrooms
½ ounce Chinese dried wood
  ears (black fungus)
4 cups chicken or vegetable
  stock
1 pound *soft* beancurd, cut
  into ½-inch cubes
4 tablespoons finely chopped
  scallions
3 tablespoons Chinese rice
  wine or dry sherry
2 tablespoons light soy sauce
2 teaspoons chili oil
½ teaspoon salt
Rice cake (page 78)
2 cups peanut oil, for deep-
  frying

GARNISH
fresh coriander leaves

 Serves 4

This soup delights not only the eye, the nose, and the palate, but also the ear as well. I always enjoy making it because, as well as the sizzling drama, it is full of flavor and easy to do. The ingredients are simple, requiring little preparation, much of which can be done ahead of time. Rice cakes are easy to make, once you have prepared them a few times. The key point to remember is that the oil used for deep-frying the pieces must be *very* hot to ensure that they become very crispy and not greasy—almost like dried popcorn. While the soup itself reheats well, the rice cake pieces must be deep-fried just before serving. ■

In separate bowls, soak the dried mushrooms and wood ears in warm water for 20 minutes. Drain them and squeeze out any excess liquid. Trim off the tough stalks and shred the mushroom caps and wood ears into 2-inch strips.

Bring the stock to a simmer in a large saucepan. Add the remaining soup ingredients, setting aside the rice cake and oil for deep-frying. Simmer for 20 minutes before transferring the soup to a large serving bowl.

Meanwhile, heat the oil in a large frying pan or a wok until it is nearly smoking. Drop in a grain of rice to test the heat—the rice should bubble all over and immediately come up to the surface.

Cut the rice cakes into pieces and deep-fry for about 1 to 2 minutes until they puff up and brown slightly. Remove immediately with a slotted spoon and drain on paper towel. Quickly transfer the pieces to a platter and slide them into the soup. It should sizzle dramatically. Garnish the soup with the fresh coriander leaves and serve at once.

Rice cake

1 cup long-grain white rice
2 cups water
2 teaspoons peanut oil

 Makes a 9-inch rice cake

Wash the rice and put into a 9- to 9½-inch wide, heavy saucepan with the water. Bring the water to the boil over high heat. Turn the heat down as low as possible, cover and cook the rice for about 45 minutes. The rice should form a heavy crust on the base of the pan. Remove all the loose surface rice, leaving the thick crust. (This loose rice can be used for making any of the Fried Rice recipes in Chapter 8.)

Dribble the oil evenly over the top of the rice cake and cook over a very low heat for 5 minutes. The cake should lift off easily at this point. If it is still sticky, add another teaspoon of oil and continue to cook until the whole cake comes loose. Put the cake onto a plate until required.

Once cooked, it can be left at room temperature for several days. Do *not* cover the rice cake as moisture will form and make it soggy. Let the rice cake dry out. It is then ready to be cut into several pieces, deep-fried, and put into the Sizzling Rice Soup (see previous recipe). As a simple snack, break it into chunks and eat hot with a sprinkling of salt.

INDONESIAN CAULIFLOWER SOUP

1 pound cauliflower

1 tablespoon peanut oil

1 tablespoon finely chopped garlic

1 small onion, finely chopped

1½ teaspoon salt

¼ teaspoon freshly ground black pepper

1 teaspoon ground coriander

2 teaspoons ground cumin

1 quart chicken or vegetable stock

¼ pound dried or fresh egg noodles

GARNISH

1 tablespoon finely chopped fresh coriander

 Serves 2 to 4

Cauliflower is a delicately flavored vegetable with a firm texture. In a soup such as this, it retains its pleasing characteristics while combining well with the distinctive flavors of coriander and cumin. The egg noodles add substance to the dish.

In its original Indonesian version, the soup is usually made with beef stock, but I prefer the lighter chicken or vegetable stock. Served with fresh bread (toasted perhaps) and a green salad, this hearty soup is a meal in itself. ■

Cut the cauliflower into florets about 1 to 1½ inches wide.

Heat a wok or large frying-pan and add the oil. Put in the garlic, onion, ½ teaspoon of the salt, pepper, coriander, and cumin and stir-fry for 2 minutes. Add the stock and cauliflower and simmer the mixture for 20 minutes or until the cauliflower is cooked.

Add the noodles to the simmering soup and cook for 8 to 10 minutes for dried noodles or 4 to 5 minutes for fresh noodles.

Add the remaining salt and give the soup a good stir. Transfer to a soup tureen and serve at once garnished with the coriander.

SPINACH AND EGG-RIBBON SOUP

¼ pound fresh spinach

1 quart dashi (page 22), or
chicken or vegetable stock

2 eggs, beaten

1 teaspoon fresh ginger juice
(page 23)

1 teaspoon salt

1 tablespoon sake, rice wine,
or dry sherry

1 teaspoon cornstarch mixed
with 1 teaspoon water

 Serves 4

When a soup appears as beautiful as it tastes, it is safe to assume a Japanese influence, as with this light soup. Try to make it with the Japanese dashi, which is essential for the authentic flavor; but if it is not available, a good chicken or vegetable stock produces a fine soup. The attractive "egg-ribbons" are made by pulling or stretching the egg strands with a fork or chopsticks as you pour them slowly into the soup. ■

Remove the stalks of the spinach and wash the leaves well. Blanch them for a few seconds in a pan of boiling water until they are just wilted. Freshen the leaves in cold water to prevent further cooking.

Put the stock into a saucepan and bring it to a simmer. Lightly beat the eggs and combine them with the ginger juice. Add the salt, sake, and blended cornstarch to the simmering stock, and stir to mix well. Pour in the egg mixture in a very slow, thin stream. Using a chopstick or fork, pull the egg slowly into strands. Drain the spinach and add to the hot soup before serving.

Corn and ginger soup

1½ pounds fresh corn on the
  cob, or 14 ounces canned
  corn, plain
1 egg, beaten
½ teaspoon sesame oil
1 tablespoon peanut oil
1 tablespoon finely chopped
  fresh ginger
1 quart chicken or vegetable
  stock
2 tablespoons rice wine or
  dry sherry
⅔ cup milk
2 teaspoons salt
½ teaspoon freshly ground
  white pepper
1 tablespoon sugar

GARNISH
1 tablespoon scallions

 Serves 4 to 6

Corn soup with crab or chicken has become a very popular dish in many Chinese restaurants in the West. It is not truly Chinese but rather reflects a blend of Eastern and Western traditions. Here is my version of the soup, a lighter vegetarian one that contains the zest of fresh ginger to enliven it. I prefer to use fresh corn, as I find the starch used in the canned variety tends to make the soup heavy. The milk in the recipe is definitely borrowed from the Western tradition; for a richer taste, use cream. This is an elegant first course for any dinner party. ■

If you are using fresh corn, remove the kernels with a sharp knife or cleaver—you should end up with about 2 cups of corn. Mix the egg and sesame oil together in a small bowl and set aside.

Heat a large saucepan until it is moderately hot. Add the oil and ginger and stir-fry for 30 seconds. Add the rest of the ingredients except the corn, egg mixture, and scallions. Bring the mixture to the boil and add the corn. Simmer for 15 minutes, uncovered, and then allow it to cool slightly.

Purée the soup in a blender or food mill until light and creamy. Return the soup to the pan and bring to a slow simmer. Add the egg mixture, stirring all the time. For serving, transfer the soup to a tureen or individual bowls and garnish with the scallions.

Steamed vegetable soup

1 ounce Chinese dried
  mushrooms
4 ounces Chinese white
  radish
4 ounces fresh or canned
  water chestnuts
2 eggs, beaten
1 teaspoon salt
1 teaspoon sesame oil
1 tablespoon peanut oil
1 quart chicken or vegetable
  stock

GARNISH

watercress leaves

 Serves 4 to 6

This is one of my favorite soups. In China, it is called "double-boiled" or "double-steamed," the name deriving from the cooking technique employed. The prepared ingredients are put in a casserole containing a boiling stock; then the casserole is sealed and placed in a steamer— a double cooking process that creates a flavorful soup. It is popular among all Chinese, and in Hong Kong it is made from various ingredients such as shark fins, pigeons, bird's nests, chicken, and, as in this recipe, vegetables. Because vegetables cook quickly, this takes little more than a half an hour to cook to full flavor, and the result is a clear soup, rather like a rich consommé. It makes a splendid first course for dinner parties or can be served as part of a family meal. ∎

Soak the dried mushrooms in warm water for 20 minutes until they are soft. Squeeze the excess liquid from the mushrooms and remove and discard their stalks. Leave the caps whole.

Peel and cut the Chinese radish into 3-inch long pieces. If you are using fresh water chestnuts, peel them; if you are using canned water chestnuts, drain well and rinse in cold water. Thinly slice the water chestnuts. Beat the eggs, ½ teaspoon of the salt, and the sesame oil together in a small bowl.

Heat a wok or frying pan until hot and add the oil. Pour in the egg mixture and cook until it sets. Remove the omelette and allow to cool. Cut it into ½-inch shreds.

Set a rack into a wok or deep pan. Fill it with 2½ inches of water and bring it to a boil. Bring the stock to a boil in another large pan and then pour the stock into a heatproof glass or china casserole. Add the radish, water chestnuts, egg shreds, mushrooms, and remaining salt to the stock. Cover and put the casserole on the rack, then cover the wok or deep pan tightly with a lid or foil. You now have a casserole within a steamer, hence the name "double-boil." Reduce the heat and steam gently for 35 minutes or until the radish is cooked. Replenish the hot water from time to time. An alternative method is to simply simmer the soup very slowly in a conventional pan, but the resulting taste will be quite different.

When the soup is cooked, it can be served immediately or cooled and stored in the refrigerator or freezer to be reheated when required. Garnish the soup with the watercress just before serving.

Japanese Seaweed Soup

3 sheets 6 x 8 inches dried
   wakame seaweed
1 quart dashi or chicken or
   vegetable stock
Rind of one lemon or lime,
   cut into thin matchsticks
½ teaspoon salt
2 tablespoons light soy sauce

Serves 4

This light rather austere soup is typical of Japanese cookery. Seaweed is high in protein and evokes the essence of the sea, and as nothing should mask this delicate rich flavor, the soup is kept very simple. The dried seaweed is well worth the search. Once the stock is made and the seaweed soaked, the receipe can be quickly put together in a matter of minutes. ■

Soak the seaweed for 20 minutes in warm water or until soft. Drain and cut it into thin shreds.

Bring the stock to a simmer in a large saucepan. Add the lemon rind, salt, and light soy and continue to simmer for another 2 minutes. Remove the soup from the heat and add the seaweed. Serve at once.

Fiery sichuan soup

2 ounces bean thread
   (transparent) noodles
½ ounce Chinese dried
   mushrooms
½ ounce Chinese dried cloud
   ears (black fungus)
½ cup bamboo shoots,
   shredded
1 egg, beaten
2 teaspoons sesame oil
1 quart chicken or vegetable
   stock
1 tablespoon finely chopped
   fresh ginger
2 tablespoons tomato paste
1 tablespoon light soy sauce
2 tablespoons dark soy sauce
2 teaspoons chili oil
1 tablespoon black rice
   vinegar or cider vinegar
2 teaspoons freshly ground
   black pepper

GARNISH

3 tablespoons finely chopped
   scallions

 Serves 4

One of the great virtues of Chinese and most Asian cuisines is their adaptability when confronted with new influences. This hot and spicy soup, now so popular in the West, is traditionally made with pork but, when dried mushrooms and cloud ears (black fungus) are substituted, the soup retains its excellent qualities and remains a substantial and nutritious meal. Do try to obtain the dried mushrooms and cloud ears—their textures are quite special. ▪

Soak the noodles in a large bowl of warm water for 15 minutes. When soft, drain them and discard the water. Cut the noodles into 3-inch lengths using scissors or a knife.

Soak the dried mushrooms and cloud ears in separate bowls of warm water for 20 minutes until soft. Squeeze the excess liquid from the mushrooms and remove and discard the stalks. Rinse the cloud ears in cold water, drain well, and leave whole. Shred the mushroom caps finely. Finely shred the bamboo shoots. Beat the eggs and sesame oil together in a small bowl.

Bring the stock to a simmer in a large pan. Add the mushrooms, cloud ears, bamboo shoots, noodles, and the rest of the ingredients, except the egg mixture and scallions. Simmer together for 5 minutes.

Finally, pour the beaten egg mixture into the soup in a steady stream. Pull the egg into strands with a fork or chopsticks. Garnish with scallions and pour the soup into a large tureen or individual bowls. Serve at once.

Fragrant noodle soup

½ pound dried or fresh egg
noodles
1 quart chicken or vegetable
stock
2 tablespoons finely chopped
scallions
1 tablespoon finely chopped
fresh coriander
½ cup celery, finely chopped
2 teaspoons sesame oil
1 tablespoon chili oil
1 tablespoon fish sauce
1 tablespoon lime juice
1 tablespoon light soy sauce
2 teaspoons sugar

 Serves 2 to 4

Egg noodles are a simple and comforting food, plain, homey, nutritious, and satisfying. Combined with soup, their virtues are magnified and when we add a touch of Southeast Asian zest—lime juice and fish sauce—the result is a wholesome soup that can serve as a light lunch for two or as a soup starter for any meal. ▪

If you are using fresh noodles, blanch them for 3 to 5 minutes in a large pan of boiling water, then immerse in cold water. If you are using dried noodles, cook in boiling water for 4 to 5 minutes. Drain the noodles, cool in cold water until required.

Put the stock into a pot and bring it to a simmer. Add the rest of the ingredients and simmer for 5 minutes. Drain the noodles and add them to the soup. Bring the soup back to simmering and serve at once.

SOUTHEAST ASIAN VEGETABLE SOUP

¼ pound carrots
¼ pound zucchini
¼ pound potatoes
¼ pound Chinese long beans,
   runner beans, or haricot
   vert, trimmed
¼ pound Chinese cabbage
2 tablespoons peanut oil
2 tablespoons finely chopped
   garlic
2 tablespoons finely chopped
   fresh lemongrass
2½ cups onions, finely
   chopped
2 teaspoons turmeric
2 tablespoons curry paste
3¾ cups chicken or vegetable
   stock
2 cups fresh or canned
   coconut milk (page 20)
1 tablespoon salt

 *Serves 4 to 6*

I have savored the fragrance and taste of curry ever since I was a small child. It was quite a surprise to me when I discovered that curry is based on Indian and not Chinese inventiveness. Here is a vegetable soup which is raised by its seasonings above the ordinary into something rather special; it is the curry which dominates (without suffocating) the other flavors. ∎

Peel and cut the carrots into 1-inch rounds. Slice the zucchini into rounds ¼ inch thick, or roll-cut them (page 42). Peel and cut the potatoes into 1-inch cubes. Trim and cut the beans into 3-inch pieces. Cut the cabbage into 1-inch chunks.

Heat the oil in a large saucepan until hot. Add the garlic, lemongrass, and onions and cook for about 2 minutes. Stir in the tumeric and curry paste and continue to cook for another 2 minutes. Add the vegetables, stock, coconut milk, and salt. Simmer for 8 minutes or until the vegetables are cooked through.

CREAMY EGGPLANT AND TOMATO SOUP

¾ pound eggplant
½ pound fresh or canned
   tomatoes
1 large onion
1 fresh chili, seeded
3 cups chicken or vegetable
   stock
2 cups fresh or canned
   coconut milk (page 20)
2 tablespoons peanut oil
2 tablespoons finely chopped
   garlic
2 teaspoons sugar
2 teaspoons salt, or to taste
½ teaspoon freshly ground
   white pepper

 Serves 4 to 6

This soup is of Indonesian origin. Eggplants are a popular vegetable throughout Southeast Asia, deriving from the white-skinned egg-shaped variety common in India. In this recipe, tomatoes (a relatively recent adaptation) are combined with coconut milk (a traditional ingredient) in a vegetable or chicken stock to create a nutritious soup that is hearty without being heavy. ■

Peel and cut the eggplant into ½-inch cubes. If you are using fresh tomatoes, peel, seed, and cut them into 1-inch cubes. If you are using canned tomatoes, cut them into small chunks. Finely chop the onion and chili.

Bring the stock and the coconut milk to a simmer in a large saucepan. While simmering, heat a wok or large frying pan and add the oil. When hot, put in the onion, chili, and eggplant and stir fry over high heat for about 4 minutes until nicely browned. Drain on paper towel, then add to the soup. Add the rest of the ingredients and simmer for 5 minutes.

Cold Dishes & Salads

Many Asian dishes contain spices and flavorings that make them delicious whether they are served hot or cold. Coldness tends to blunt the taste of spices and seasonings, hence you can use more of them in cold dishes. In China, there is a lively tradition of serving intricately designed cold food platters at banquets and other special occasions. This is no accident. When food is to be served cold, it is naturally prepared well ahead of time, making it perfect for large gatherings and buffets and, in our day, for picnics. Cold dishes also make warm weather dining more agreeable and pleasant.

Raw vegetable salads are almost unknown in Asia. There, food is always cooked at least a little before it is deemed ready for a sauce or dressing. There are several reasons for this, most notably reasons of hygiene. Brief cooking destroys any bacteria or tiny insects in the vegetables that could be harmful. In traditional societies without a supply of clean water, the eating of raw foods is often unwise; warm weather with no refrigeration contributes to the rapid growth of bacteria, also a potential danger. Quick cooking renders food both safe and more easily digestible.

You will find many of these dishes blend well with your everyday meals. For example, the Peppery Eggplant makes a delicious family starter, or serve Asparagus with Tangy Mustard Dressing at a dinner party.

PEPPERY EGGPLANT

1 pound eggplant

SAUCE

1½ teaspoons Sichuan
    peppercorns, roasted and
    ground (page 31)
1½ teaspoons salt
1 teaspoon sugar
2 tablespoons sesame oil
6 tablespoons finely chopped
    scallion tops
2 teaspoons finely chopped
    fresh coriander
1 tablespoon Chinese white
    rice vinegar or cider
    vinegar.

Serves 4

India and the Far East consume the greatest quantities of eggplants. This is to be expected, for although this splendid vegetable is not cultivated in warm climates throughout the world, its homeland is India. It has been a traditional food in Eastern cookery for many centuries. This recipe was inspired by my good friend, Hwang San, in his delightful Hunan-style restaurant, Dong Ting, in Houston, Texas. He steams the eggplant, but I find roasting them just as easy with the same results. Eggplants have a very spongy texture and can absorb a great deal of oil when they are fried or even stir-fried.

This dish works well as an appetizer. The cooked eggplant is not too filling and the peppercorn sauce stimulates the palate. Because this dish may be made well ahead of time, it is quite practical for entertaining. It is an excellent picnic dish too. ■

Preheat the oven to 400°F. If you are using Chinese eggplants, roast for 20 minutes; if you are using large eggplant, roast for about 30 to 40 minutes or until they are soft to the touch and cooked through. Allow the eggplant to cool and then peel.

Arrange the eggplant on a platter. Combine the sauce ingredients, pour over the eggplant, and serve at once.

Hot and sour cucumber salad

1 pound cucumbers
¼ cup white rice or cider
  vinegar
1 tablespoon sugar
1 teaspoon salt
½ ounce fresh red chili, finely
  sliced
1 teaspoon finely chopped
  garlic

Serves 4

In Thailand, the cucumbers are shorter and thicker than our Western variety. They also are fairly bursting with seeds. But no matter, for whatever type we use, the cucumber's mild flavor and juicy crunchiness comes through. In this recipe, cucumbers are marinated in a piquant vinegary dressing, making them an ideal accompaniment to any fried or grilled dishes. They may also be served as a salad in their own right. By all means experiment: you may find you enjoy an even spicier version. Just add more chilies and garlic. ▪

Slice the cucumbers in half lengthways and, using a teaspoon, remove the seeds. Cut the cucumber halves into 3-inch by ½-inch pieces.

Combine the cucumber pieces with the rest of the ingredients in a bowl and allow them to marinate for at least 4 hours or more in the refrigerator, stirring them from time to time. When you are ready to serve, drain them thoroughly.

SPINACH IN OYSTER SAUCE

1½ pounds fresh spinach

SAUCE
1½ tablespoons oyster sauce
2 teaspoons sesame oil
2 teaspoons sugar

 *Serves 2 to 4*

Spinach is a nutritious vegetable with a fine flavor. The trend through-out the West is to consume more and more fresh spinach instead of canned or frozen, and spinach leaves are increasingly used in salads. This recipe is based on a traditional southern Chinese method but, instead of serving the cooked spinach warm, I serve it cold. In the area around Canton, there is a variety called water spinach, which has a milder taste and which, when cooked, presents a pleasing contrast between the crunchy stalk and soft leaves. It may sometimes be found at Asian specialty stores, and I encourage you to look for it to try, but ordinary fresh spinach will do very well. ■

Remove the stalks from the spinach and wash the leaves well. Blanch the leaves for a few seconds in a saucepan of boiling water until just wilted. Remove and freshen them in cold water to prevent further cooking. Drain the leaves in a colander, then place them on a linen towel and gently squeeze out all the excess liquid. Arrange on a serv-ing dish.

Mix the sauce ingredients together and pour over the spinach. This dish can remain at room temperature until ready to serve.

East-West shredded salad

¼ pound carrots
1 ounce fresh chilies
   (optional)
4 scallions
½ pound iceberg lettuce
¼ pound bean sprouts

DRESSING

1 tablespoon finely chopped
   fresh ginger
2 dried chilies, chopped
3 tablespoons finely chopped
   scallions
½ teaspoon Sichuan
   peppercorns, roasted and
   ground (page 31)
1 tablespoon light soy sauce
1 tablespoon Chinese white
   rice vinegar or cider
   vinegar
2 tablespoons peanut oil
2 teaspoons sesame oil

 Serves 2 to 4

Raw or almost raw vegetables are enjoyed in most countries both East and West, but not in China where they are usually at least stir-fired, blanched, or pickled. I enjoy raw vegetables, thus showing my Western culinary influences, but I understand my Chinese preference also. Hence, this East-West compromise: delicious, fresh, raw vegetables covered with a heated zesty Chinese-inspired sauce that coats the salad. The result pleases both eye and palate and creates a refreshing salad for any meal. ■

Peel and cut the carrots into 2-inch fine shreds. Cut the chilies, scallions, and lettuce into 2-inch fine shreds. In a large bowl, mix all the vegetables together.

    Combine all the dressing ingredients, except the oils, in a heatproof bowl. Heat the oils in a small saucepan or wok until almost smoking. Pour the hot oils over the dressing ingredients and allow to cool for 5 minutes. Pour the dressing over the vegetables and toss thoroughly. Serve at once.

Sesame-dressed Spinach Salad

1½ pounds fresh spinach
1 teaspoon toasted sesame
   seeds (page 30)

DRESSING

½ teaspoon salt
1½ tablespoons light soy
   sauce
2 teaspoons sugar
2 teaspoons Chinese white
   rice vinegar or cider
   vinegar
1 tablespoon peanut oil

 *Serves 2 to 4*

Spinach is used extensively in Japanese, Chinese, and Indonesian cooking. I have often enjoyed this spinach salad in Japanese restaurants in Asia, and I was pleased to learn how simple it is to make. In Japan, spinach is picked when it is still quite a small plant; this assures a sweet and tender leaf. The essential technique is to blanch the spinach quickly, plunge it into cold water (to stop the cooking and preserve the deep color) and to squeeze out all excess liquid. The spinach is then ready to absorb the flavors of the marinade. ■

Wash the spinach thoroughly and remove the stalks. Blanch the leaves in a saucepan of boiling salted water for about 30 seconds. Drain and immerse the leaves in cold water. Drain in a colander. Put the spinach inside a clean linen towel and gently squeeze out all the excess liquid.

Combine all the dressing ingredients in a small bowl and mix thoroughly. Combine the spinach and dressing and let the salad marinate in the dressing for at least 1½ hours before serving, or refrigerate and serve within 3 hours. Sprinkle the toasted sesame seeds on the top just before serving.

Bean sprout salad

1 pound fresh bean sprouts
1 fresh red chili, seeded and
    finely shredded

DRESSING

1½ tablespoons light soy
    sauce
1 teaspoon peanut oil
2 teaspoons sesame oil
1 teaspoon chili oil
1 teaspoon finely chopped
    garlic
2 tablespoons finely chopped
    scallions
½ teaspoon sugar
½ teaspoon salt
¼ teaspoon freshly ground
    white pepper

 Serves 4

Bean sprouts have been enjoyed in China and Southeast Asia for centuries but have only recently been introduced to the West. They are essentially a transitional food, as it were, midway between the seed or bean from which they spring and the vegetable they will become. They have significant nutritional value, a nutty flavor, and crisp texture as well. Mung beans and soybeans are the favored sprouts among the Chinese, who love them cooked but never in raw form. Lightly blanched, as in this recipe, the sprouts lose their raw taste but retain their crispness and flavor. This salad is easily made and can be prepared hours in advance of need. Refreshing and spicy, it goes well with grilled meats. ■

Trim and discard both ends of the bean sprouts. Blanch the bean sprouts in a large saucepan of boiling water for 1 minute. Drain in a colander, immerse them in cold water, then drain again.

    Combine the dressing ingredients in a small bowl. Mix the dressing together with the sprouts and the chili.

CHINESE EGGPLANT SALAD

1 pound eggplant

<u>DRESSING</u>

2 tablespoons finely chopped
   scallions
2 teaspoons chili oil
2 teaspoons fish sauce
1 tablespoon light soy sauce
1 teaspoon finely chopped
   garlic

 Serves 4

Fish sauce makes a piquant dressing for this eggplant salad. Roasting the eggplant preserves the moist, sweet flavors. Quickly made, this dish can be served warm or cold. ■

Preheat the oven to 400°F. If you are using Chinese eggplant, roast for 20 minutes; if you are using the large eggplant, roast for about 30 to 40 minutes or until soft and cooked through. Allow to cool, then peel. Cut the eggplant meat into strips.

Arrange the eggplant on a platter. Combine the dressing ingredients and pour over the eggplant. Serve the salad immediately or refrigerate and serve the next day.

COLD GREEN BEAN SALAD

½ pound Chinese long beans, runner beans, or haricot vert, trimmed
1 tablespoon peanut oil
1 small onion, finely chopped

DRESSING

1 tablespoon fish sauce
2 teaspoons toasted sesame seeds (page 30)
2 tablespoons lemon juice
2 teaspoons sesame oil
1 teaspoon salt
2 teaspoons chili oil

 *Serves 2 to 4*

Simplicity itself, this recipe takes a favorite vegetable and gives it a touch of Southeast Asian zest. The fish sauce is commonly used in many parts of Southeast Asia and, when combined with other spices, will enliven any dish. Serve these beans either as a salad or as a side vegetable dish. They may be prepared well ahead of time. ■

If you are using Chinese long beans or runner beans, cut them into 3-inch lengths. If you are using haricot vert, leave whole. Blanch the beans in a large saucepan of boiling salted water for 2 minutes. Immerse them in cold water, drain thoroughly, and set aside.

Heat a wok or frying pan and add the oil. When moderately hot, add the onion and stir-fry for 2 minutes and then allow to cool. Add to the beans.

Combine all the dressing ingredients and toss with the beans and onions. Serve the salad immediately or refrigerate and serve the next day.

CRISPY NOODLE SALAD

1¼ cups peanut oil, for deep
    frying
¼ pound rice noodles, rice
    vermicelli, or rice sticks

SAUCE

2 cloves garlic, crushed
2 tablespoons finely chopped
    shallots
3 tablespoons fish sauce
1 tablespoon sugar
2 tablespoons Chinese white
    vinegar or cider vinegar

GARNISH

¼ pound firm bean curd, cut
    into small dice
½ pound bean sprouts
3 scallions, shredded
1 fresh chili, shredded
fresh coriander springs

 Serves 4

I first enjoyed this salad, called Mee Krob, in a rather unpretentious restaurant in Bangkok. There are a number of different variations on the crispy noodle salad theme, with many people preferring a sweet and sour salad. At home, I set out to recreate the combination of textures, flavors, and colors that had most impressed me in Thailand, and this recipe is my favorite—a beautifully arranged salad platter that is dressed and tossed at the last minute. Such a salad is ideal as a beginning to any meal. ▪

Heat the oil in a deep-fat fryer or wok until moderately hot. Deep-fry the noodles until crispy and puffed up. Remove from the oil with a slotted spoon and drain on paper towel. You may have to do this in several batches. (Leave the oil in the deep-fat fryer or wok as you will need it for the bean curd.)

Cut the bean curd into ½-inch cubes. Reheat the oil until very hot and deep-fry the bean curd cubes until golden. Remove with a slotted spoon and drain on paper towel.

Combine the sauce ingredients in a small bowl and mix well.

Place the crispy noodles on a serving platter and garnish attractively with the bean curd, bean sprouts, scallions, chili, and coriander. Pour the dressing over the salad just before serving and mix well.

Asparagus with tangy mustard dressing

1 pound fresh asparagus

<u>DRESSING</u>

1 teaspoon dried mustard
1 teaspoon hot water
1 egg yolk
1 tablespoon dark soy sauce
1 teaspoon finely chopped
  fresh ginger
¼ teaspoon salt

 *Serves 2 to 4*

Asparagus is a relative newcomer to the cast of vegetables in Asian cuisine, but there is no doubt it has won a permanent starring role in the repertory. Its popularity is based on contrasts: properly cooked, it has a firm but soft texture, a delicate yet earthy, assertive flavor—and a brilliant color. In this Japanese-style recipe, the asparagus is simply cooked by quickly blanching, the briefest processing possible. The mustard-ginger dressing only highlights and never intrudes upon the taste of the asparagus. Since asparagus is relatively expensive, indulge yourself and savor this recipe when it is in season. Serve it as an appetizer or a side dish to any meal. ■

Break off the woody ends of the asparagus and cut the stalks into 3-inch diagonal pieces. Blanch the asparagus in a large saucepan of boiling salted water for 2 minutes. Plunge them into cold water, then drain in a colander. Pat them dry with paper towel.

In a small bowl, mix the mustard and hot water together and stir until it is a thick paste. Add the rest of the dressing ingredients and mix well.

Arrange the asparagus on a serving platter and pour the dressing over. Serve immediately or within 3 hours.

GREEN AND WHITE JADE SALAD

½ pound broccoli
½ pound cauliflower

DRESSING

2 tablespoons sesame paste or
  peanut butter
1 tablespoon Chinese white
  rice vinegar or cider
  vinegar
1 teaspoon chili oil
1 teaspoon sesame oil
1 tablespoon light soy sauce
1 teaspoon salt
2 teaspoons sugar

 Serves 2 to 4

White and green jade bring luck, or so Asian people believe. Lacking the real thing, this broccoli and cauliflower treat does very nicely, and brings pleasure and nourishment with it. This is a delicious and color-ful warm weather dish and is fine as an appetizer or to carry on pic-nics. The well-flavored dressing is equally delicious with other vegetable combinations, such as carrots and Brussels sprouts. ■

Cut off the broccoli heads and break them into small florets. Peel the broccoli stalks if necessary and slice. Cut the cauliflower into small florets, about 1 to 1½ inches wide. Blanch the broccoli heads, stalks, and cauliflower in a large saucepan of boiling salted water for 4 min-utes. Plunge them into cold water, then drain. Dry the broccoli and cauliflower in a colander or a salad spinner and arrange on a platter.

Mix the dressing ingredients together in a bowl or a blender. (This can be done in advance and kept refrigerated as the sauce should be cold.) Pour the dressing over the vegetables and serve.

Vegetables

Vegetables are important in any cuisine that is nutritious, flavorful, and colorful. In the Cantonese cuisine of south China, considered among the most nutritious in the world, more vegetables of diverse texture, shape, size, and color are used than in almost any other culinary tradition. My mother, who is of Cantonese origin, consequently relied heavily on vegetables in our home-cooking. She used traditional Chinese vegetables whenever they were available, but she reached out to harvest the Western cornucopia as well. In Chinese cookery, technique is more important than even the ingredients. My mother took standard European vegetables and prepared them so well that, unlike my Western schoolmates, I loved to eat them. As my mother cooked them, the vegetables retained their fresh flavors, textures, nutritious vitamins, and colors.

Many vegetables have delicate textures; most of them have only subtle flavors. How does one cook them and yet preserve their qualities? Well, practice makes perfect, especially to avoid overcooking. With vegetables, you need to nibble, taste, nibble, taste as you cook. Below are a few guidelines I have found helpful:

If vegetables in the raw state are soft, leafy, delicate, and full of moisture, like spinach, Chinese greens, and lettuce, they need very little cooking. A simple blanching or quick stir-frying in a little oil with intense heat will cook them to perfection. Stir-frying at high heat seals in their moisture and flavors; low heat will steam them and draw out moisture leaving them dry with an overcooked taste and appearance. If you blanch these vegetables, plunge them immediately afterwards in cold water to stop them from cooking; this also sets and preserves their vivid colors.

▪ Some vegetables are what I call "in-between." That is, they are not soft, like spinach, nor are they firm and crunchy like carrots. They usually contain some moisture but are crisp and thus need some cooking. I have in mind vegetables like zucchini, snow peas, red and green peppers, and cucumbers. "Salting" is usually a good technique to prepare zucchini and cucumbers for cooking. This method draws out some of their liquid while preserving their textures and flavors. Cook these vegetables a little longer than you would the more tender, leafy ones.

▪ Then there are the "hard" vegetables, such as carrots, Chinese white radish, broccoli, cauliflower and Brussels sprouts. These firm-textured vegetables usually require two separate cooking procedures—blanching, to soften them and then stir-frying to cook them sufficiently and infuse them with additional flavors. Alternatively, they can be cooked in a larger amount of liquid.

▪ Not all vegetables are meant to be cooked "just to the point." Eggplant, bitter melon, and Chinese cabbage profit from more extensive cooking. Some release additional liquid or bitter juices in the cooking process.

▪ If you are cooking a multi-vegetable dish or combining vegetables with other foods such as meat, fish, or poultry, you can cook the different vegetables separately and *then* combine everything at the last moment. The result will be perfectly cooked every time, because every element of the dish will have had its own correct cooking time.

▪ Finally, a great deal of vegetable cookery involves common sense and experience. Don't worry and trust your own judgment. If you make a mistake, it will be a valuable lesson for your next attempt.

In this book, I have included vegetable recipes from China, Japan, Korea, and Southeast Asia. The vegetables, spices, and seasonings have an Asian flavor that complements European foods. Experiment with them and include them in your everyday cooking. Some recipes include more exotic vegetables for those who are more adventurous, but most involve vegetables you can easily buy at your supermarket.

☐ BEAN SPROUTS

Bean sprouts are now widely available in supermarkets, health food stores and Asian specialty markets. They are the sprouts of the green mung bean, although some Asian specialty markets also stock yellow soybean sprouts which are much larger. Bean sprouts should always be very fresh and crunchy. They will keep for several days wrapped in a plastic bag and stored in the vegetable compartment of a refrigerator. Never use canned bean sprouts as these have been precooked and are soggy and tasteless.

To grow bean sprouts

It is very easy to grow your own bean sprouts. Dried mung beans are obtainable from supermarkets, Asian specialty markets and health food shops. You will need to obtain or devise a perforated flat surface. An aluminum foil pan punched with holes or a bamboo steamer are both ideal. You will also need 2 pieces of cheesecloth and 1 ounce dried green mung beans.

Wash the beans several times in water, then leave them to soak in lukewarm water for 8 hours or overnight. Once soaking is complete, rinse the beans again under warm running water until the water runs clear. Dampen the cheesecloth and spread one piece over the aluminum pan or steamer. Spread the beans over the cloth and sprinkle them with more lukewarm water. Cover the beans with the second piece of cheesecloth and then put them in a warm dark place. Keep them moist by sprinkling with water over the next few days. In 3 days you should have white crisp sprouts.

- **BITTER MELON** Used as a vegetable, bitter melon has a strong flavor worthy of its name. The greener the melon, the more bitter its taste, so many cooks look for the milder yellow-green skinned melon. To use, cut in half, seed, and discard the interior membrane. To lessen the bitter taste, either blanch or salt according to the instructions in the recipe.

- **CHINESE BROCCOLI** Chinese broccoli or gai lan (*Brassica oleracea capitata*) does not taste like European broccoli (calabrese). It is very crunchy, slightly bitter, and resembles Swiss chard in flavor. It has deep olive green leaves and sometimes has white flowers. Chinese broccoli is usually only available at Asian specialty markets. If you can find it, look for firm stalks and leaves which look fresh and green. Prepared exactly the same way as broccoli, it should be stored in a plastic bag in the vegetable compartment of the refrigerator where it will keep for several days. If you cannot find Chinese broccoli, substitute ordinary broccoli instead.

- **CHINESE CABBAGE** Chinese cabbage (*Brassica pekinensis*) looks rather like a large, tightly packed Romaine lettuce with firm, pale green, crinkled leaves. It is sometimes known as Napa, Peking, or celery cabbage and is widely available from supermarkets and Asian specialty markets. This is a delicious crunchy vegetable with a mild but distinctive taste. If you cannot find it, use white cabbage instead.

- **CHINESE CHIVES** Chinese chives are related to common chives, but their taste is much stronger and garlic-like, and their flowers can be used as well as the blades. Chinese chives can be found in Asian specialty markets but are very easy to grow in home herb gardens. Look for wide flat blades and sprays of white, star-shaped flowers. They can be substituted for ordinary chives but adjust the quantity to allow for their stronger flavor. Rinse and dry the chives, store them in a plastic bag in the refrigerator, and use as soon as possible.

⊡ CHINESE FLOWERING CABBAGE

Chinese flowering cabbage (*Brassica rapa*) is usually known by its more familiar Cantonese name, choi sam. It has yellowish green leaves and may have small yellow flowers which are eaten along with the leaves and stems. It is obtainable from Asian specialty markets and is delicious stir-fried.

⊡ CHINESE GREENS

Chinese greens (*Brassica chinensis*) is an attractive vegetable with a long, smooth, milky-white stalk and large, crinkly, dark green leaves. It is similar to Swiss chard, and has been grown for centuries in China, where it is known as bok choi. In the West, it is sometimes called Chinese white cabbage or Chinese chard, and it has a light fresh taste and requires little cooking. It is usually available from supermarkets and Asian specialty markets. Swiss chard or spinach can be substituted if you cannot obtain Chinese greens.

⊡ CHINESE LONG BEANS

Also known as yard-long beans, Chinese long beans (*Vigna sesquipedalis*) can grow to about 3 feet in length. Although runner beans and haricot vert can be substituted for the long beans, they are not related, the long beans having originated in Asia. Buy beans with fresh bright green texture and no dark marks. You will usually find beans sold in looped bunches. Store the beans in a plastic bag in the refrigerator and use within 4 days.

⊡ CHINESE WHITE RADISH

Chinese white radish is long and white and rather like a carrot in shape but usually very much larger. A winter radish or root, it can withstand long cooking without disintegrating, so it absorbs the flavor of a sauce yet retains its distinctive radish taste and texture. It must be peeled before use. Chinese white radish can be bought in many supermarkets, produce stores, and in Asian specialty markets. They should be firm, heavy, and unblemished, slightly translucent inside, and not tough or fibrous. Store in a plastic bag in the vegetable compartment of your refrigerator where they will keep for over a week. If you cannot find white radish, use turnips instead.

⊡ EGGPLANT

These smooth purple-skinned vegetables range in size from the huge fat ones which are easy to find in all supermarkets to the small thin variety which the Chinese prefer because they have a more delicate flavor.

Asians do not normally peel eggplants since the skin preserves their texture, shape, and taste. Large eggplants should be cut according to the recipe, sprinkled with a little salt, and left to stand for 20 minutes. They should then be rinsed and any liquid blotted dry with paper towel. This process extracts excess moisture and bitter juices from the vegetable before it is cooked.

⊡ LEEKS

Resembling a giant scallion, leeks (*Allium porrum*) have a mild onion flavor. To use, cut off and discard the green tops and roots and slice the leek in half lengthwise. Wash them well. Use as directed in the recipe.

⊡ SHALLOTS

Shallots are mild-flavored members of the onion family. They are small—about the size of pickling onions—with copper-red skins and a distinctive onion taste. However, they are not as strong or overpowering as ordinary onions. I think they are an excellent substitute for Chinese onions which are unobtainable here. They are expensive, but a few go a long way. Keep them in a cool, dry place (not the refrigerator) and peel them as you would an onion. If you cannot find shallots, use pickling onions or scallions.

⊡ SNOW PEAS

These tender flat green pods combine a crisp texture with a sweet, fresh flavor. Snow peas are delicious whether stir-fried with a little oil and salt, or combined with other ingredients. Shredded, they add a crisp texture and sweet taste to stuffings and other dishes. They produce a crunchy, tender, unique salad when blanched and tossed in a dressing. Before cooking, the ends should be trimmed. Snow peas are available from supermarkets and produce stores. Look for pods that are firm with very small peas, which means they are tender and young. They keep for at least a week in the vegetable compartment of the refrigerator.

⊡ SPINACH

Western varieties of spinach are quite different from those used in China, although they make satisfactory substitutes for the Asian variety. Spinach is most commonly stir-fried, so frozen spinach is obviously unsuitable. Chinese water spinach (*Ipomoea aquatica*) is available in some produce stores and in Asian specialty markets. It has hollow stems and delicate, pointed green leaves, lighter in color than common spinach and with a milder taste. It should be cooked when it is very fresh, preferably on the day on which it is bought.

⊡ WATER CHESTNUTS

Sweet, crisp white water chestnuts have been eaten in China for centuries. They are especially popular in the south, where they are sometimes grown between rice plants in paddies. (This is why they are often muddy.) They are not part of the chestnut family at all, but an edible root or bulb about the size of a chestnut that forms at the base of the stem. Canned water chestnuts are a pale version of the fresh ones, because both the crispness and the flavor are lost in the canning process. Fresh water chestnuts can sometimes be obtained from Asian specialty markets or good supermarkets and will keep unpeeled in a paper bag in the refrigerator for up to 2 weeks. Look for a firm, hard texture. The skin should be tight and taut, not wrinkled. If they are mushy, they are too old; feel them all over for soft, rotten spots. If you peel water chestnuts in advance, cover with cold water to prevent browning and store in the refrigerator.

RAINBOW VEGETABLES IN LETTUCE CUPS

1 pound iceberg lettuce
¼ pound carrots
½ pound zucchini
¼ pound red peppers
¼ pound yellow peppers
1¼ cups peanut oil for deep-frying plus 1 tablespoon peanut oil
1 ounce bean thread (transparent) noodles
3 tablespoons coarsely chopped garlic
½ teaspoon salt
2 tablespoons rice wine or dry sherry
3 tablespoons chicken or vegetable stock
¼ pound fresh or canned water chestnuts, coarsely chopped
2 teaspoons light soy sauce
1½ tablespoons oyster sauce
3 tablespoons hoisin sauce

 Serves 4 to 6

In this version of a popular Hong Kong dish, one that usually includes minced lean beef, pigeons, or pork, I use only vegetables. The meat or poultry is not missed when one savors the tasty crunchiness of the vegetables combined with crispy fried bean thread noodles, cupped in a refreshing lettuce leaf flavored with hoisin sauce. This dish makes a good appetizer for a festive meal, as guests can fill their own lettuce cups at the table. ■

Separate, wash, and dry the lettuce leaves. Finely dice the carrots, zucchini, and peppers.

In a deep-fat fryer or large wok, heat 1¼ cups of oil until almost smoking. Turn off the heat and deep-fry the noodles until they are crisp and puffed up. Drain on paper towel.

Heat a wok or large frying-pan and add 1 tablespoon of the oil in which you have fried the noodles. Put in the garlic, salt, carrots, rice wine, and stock and stir-fry for about 2 minutes. Then add the rest of the vegetables and the water chestnuts (except the lettuce) together with the soy sauce and stir-fry for 3 minutes. Stir in the oyster sauce and continue to stir-fry for 1 more minute. Turn the mixture onto a platter. Arrange the lettuce and noodles on separate platters, put the hoisin sauce in a small bowl, and serve.

Summer Pepper Stir-Fry

1 ounce Chinese dried
    mushrooms
2 eggs, beaten
1 teaspoon sesame oil
¼ teaspoon salt
2 teaspoons peanut oil
1 tablespoon finely chopped
    scallions
1 tablespoon finely chopped
    fresh ginger
1 tablespoon finely chopped
    garlic
1 small fresh chili, seeded
    and finely shredded
½ pound red, yellow, or
    green peppers (about 1
    each)
2 teaspoons rice wine or dry
    sherry
1 teaspoon light soy sauce
1 teaspoon sugar
Salt and freshly ground black
    pepper to taste
¼ pound bean sprouts,
    (preferably plucked on both
    ends)
2 teaspoons sesame oil

GARNISH

2 tablespoons finely chopped
    scallions

 Serves 2 to 4

Here is an ensemble of colors, flavors, tastes, and textures, that will appeal to the eye as well as the palate. ■

Soak the dried mushrooms in warm water for 20 minutes or until soft. Squeeze out the excess water and cut away the stalks. Shred the mushroom caps and set aside.

Combine the beaten eggs with 1 teaspoon of sesame oil and salt in a small bowl. Heat a frying-pan or wok over moderate heat and add 2 teaspoons of the peanut oil. Add the egg-mixture and spread over the surface of the pan until it forms a thin crêpe-like pancake. Remove from the heat and, when cool, cut the egg pancake into thin shreds and set aside.

Heat a wok or large frying-pan over high heat and add the remaining peanut oil. Put in the scallions, ginger, garlic, and chili and stir-fry for 30 seconds. Add the peppers, mushrooms, rice wine, soy sauce, sugar, salt, and pepper. Stir-fry for 2 minutes until the peppers are soft. Add the bean sprouts and egg shreds and stir-fry gently for another 2 minutes, then add the remaining sesame oil. Remove the mixture to a serving platter and garnish with the chopped scallions. Serve at once.

MOCK VEGETABLE PASTA

2 pounds zucchini
1 tablespoon salt
1 tablespoon peanut oil
1 tablespoon finely chopped
   garlic
2 teaspoons finely chopped
   fresh ginger
2 tablespoons finely chopped
   fresh coriander
2 tablespoons finely chopped
   scallions, green parts only

 Serves 4

In Chinese vegetarian cooking, a dish is not always what it appears to be. For example, "mock duck" is taro root stuffed with minced vegetables and fried to a golden brown to look like duck. I enjoy the fun and imaginativeness of such creativity, and here I take zucchini and cut them into long thin strips to look like pasta. I then salt them to remove excess moisture and, in the process, firm their texture. Quickly stir-fried with traditional Chinese seasonings, the resulting dish looks and tastes like pasta—my guests are always surprised by its lightness, flavor and texture. Do not overcook the zucchini—you want an "al dente" firmness to the bite. This mock pasta is also delicious cold, and it can even function as a vegetable or salad serving. It is perfect for picnics. ▪

Cut the zucchini into long thin strips resembling pasta. Put the strips into a colander and sprinkle with salt. Let them stand for 20 minutes. Then wrap the zucchini in a linen towel and gently squeeze out the excess liquid.

Heat a large frying-pan or wok over moderate heat and add the oil. Put in the garlic and ginger and stir-fry for 30 seconds. Add the zucchini, fresh coriander, and scallions and continue to stir-fry for 4 minutes or until the zucchini is thoroughly heated through. Turn the mixture onto a platter and serve warm at room temperature.

STIR-FRIED ASPARAGUS IN BLACK BEAN SAUCE

1 pound fresh asparagus

1 tablespoon peanut oil

2 teaspoons finely chopped
fresh ginger

2 teaspoons finely chopped
garlic

2 tablespoons black beans,
coarsely chopped

2 teaspoons chili bean sauce

⅔ cup chicken or vegetable
stock

1 teaspoon sugar

3 tablespoons rice wine or
dry sherry

1 teaspoon sesame oil

 Serves 2

Asparagus is expensive even when in season, but it is so exquisite a treat it is worth buying as often as you can. Not a traditional ingredient of Southeast Asian cuisines, it has been very quickly incorporated during this century. It goes well with this pungent and robust black bean sauce, a traditional Chinese seasoning. Combined with spices, this vegetarian dish can rival any expensive meat. With rice and perhaps one other light dish, this recipe forms a complete meal for two. ■

Cut the asparagus on a diagonal slant into 3-inch lengths.

Heat a wok or large frying-pan and add the oil. When hot, add the ginger, garlic, and black beans and stir-fry for a few seconds. Add the chili bean sauce and a few seconds later, add the asparagus and stir-fry for 2 minutes. Stir in the stock, sugar, and rice wine. Cook the mixture over high heat for about 2 minutes stirring continuously. Add the sesame oil, give the mixture a couple of stirs, and serve at once.

DRY-BRAISED BAMBOO SHOOTS WITH BROCCOLI

½ pound fresh broccoli

1¼ pounds bamboo shoots, canned

⅔ cup peanut oil

1 teaspoon finely chopped fresh ginger

1 teaspoon salt

1 tablespoon yellow bean sauce

1 tablespoon sugar

3 tablespoons rice wine or dry sherry

⅔ cup chicken or vegetable stock

1 tablespoon peanut oil

2 teaspoons finely chopped garlic

 Serves 4

Fresh bamboo shoots are rare outside the Asian subtropics, where they are featured in many recipes as a vegetable, as part of a stuffing, or as a garnish for meat, seafood and vegetarian dishes. They are boiled before eating because they contain a cyanide-type poison which must be broken down. I have often wondered how it was discovered that so dangerous a food could be transformed into a delicacy—who first dared to try fresh bamboo shoots? However, those of us outside of Asia must make do with the canned variety. This is unfortunate because fresh bamboo shoots are a true delicacy. The canned version is an acceptable substitute but one that requires a little work to restore the flavor lost in the canning process. Served with rice, this recipe makes a light and very appetizing vegetarian meal. ■

Separate the broccoli heads into florets, then peel the stalks if necessary and slice. Blanch all the broccoli pieces in a large saucepan of boiling, salted water for several minutes. Drain and immerse them in cold water. Drain again thoroughly in a colander and set aside. Rinse the canned bamboo shoots well.

Cut the bamboo shoots into 3-inch by ½-inch segments and dry them thoroughly with paper towel. Heat the ⅔ cup oil in a wok or a large frying-pan. Pan-fry the bamboo shoots until they are nicely brown. Drain thoroughly on paper towel and set aside.

Pour off all but 1 tablespoon of the oil and reheat the wok. Add the ginger, ½ teaspoon of the salt, and the bean sauce, and stir-fry for 1 minute. Return the bamboo shoots to the wok, add the sugar, rice wine, and stock. Braise for 3 to 5 minutes over high heat until most of the liquid has evaporated. Remove and set aside.

Wipe the wok clean, reheat and add 1 tablespoon fresh oil. When smoking slightly, add the garlic, remaining salt, and broccoli to the wok and stir-fry for 1 minute. Return the bamboo shoots to the wok and continue to stir-fry for another 2 to 3 minutes or until heated through. Turn the mixture onto a platter and serve at once.

Asparagus with Chinese Black Mushrooms

1 pound large asparagus
1 ounce Chinese dried
  mushrooms
1 tablespoon peanut oil
2 cloves garlic, lightly
  crushed
¼ teaspoon salt
⅔ cup chicken or vegetable
  stock
2 tablespoons oyster sauce
1 teaspoon cornstarch mixed
  with 1 teaspoon cold water

 Serves 2 to 4

Asparagus is a vegetable which readily combines with many other foods in the most congenial fashion. Here, it is joined with the meaty, smoky, Chinese dried mushrooms, with both vegetables absorbing the essences of each other and the sauce. I suggest that, if available, you use a larger variety of asparagus. This is a wholesome and satisfying dish, easy to prepare and, with rice, a meal in itself. ■

Cut the asparagus diagonally into 2-inch lengths, discarding the hard woody ends.

Soak the dried mushrooms in warm water for about 20 minutes. Remove the mushrooms from the water and squeeze out any excess liquid. Cut off the stalks and discard them.

Heat a wok or large frying-pan over moderate heat and add the oil. Put in the garlic, salt, and asparagus and stir-fry for 1 minute. Add the stock and mushrooms and continue to stir-fry for 3 minutes or until the asparagus is cooked. Add the oyster sauce and blended cornstarch and continue to cook until the sauce has been reduced to a glaze. Give the mixture a final stir, turn onto a platter, and serve at once.

Sichuan fried eggplant

1 pound eggplant
2 cups peanut oil for deep-
frying

BATTER

¼ cup all-purpose flour
⅔ cup water
¼ teaspoon salt

SAUCE

1 tablespoon peanut oil
3 tablespoons finely chopped
scallions
1 tablespoon finely chopped
fresh ginger
2 teaspons chili bean sauce
⅔ cup chicken or vegetable
stock
2 tablespoons rice wine or
dry sherry
1 tablespoon Chinese black
rice vinegar or cider
vinegar
3 tablespoons tomato paste
2 teaspoons sugar
2 tablespoons dark soy sauce
1 teaspoon cornstarch mixed
with 1 teaspoon water

 *Serves 4 to 6*

Eggplants are delicious when fried in a light batter, which prevents too much oil penetrating the eggplants. They are then enlivened by what the Chinese call a "fish flavoring" sauce, a non-fishy mixture of spices and seasonings normally used in the preparation of fish. Both the eggplant and the batter readily absorb the sauce. This is not to be confused with commercially bottled fish sauce widely used in Southeast Asian cooking. Try to buy the Chinese eggplants as they have a more delicate taste; however, ordinary eggplant will suffice. This is an excellent appetizer. If you serve it with cocktails, serve the sauce separately. ■

Cut the eggplant into thin 1½-inch by 3-inch slices. Do not peel them.

For the batter mix the flour, water, and salt together in a small bowl, then strain through a fine sieve. Let rest for about 20 minutes.

For the sauce, heat a wok or large frying-pan until hot and add the 1 tablespoon of oil. Put in the scallions, ginger, and chili bean sauce and stir-fry for 30 seconds. Then add the stock, rice wine, vinegar, tomato paste, sugar, and soy sauce and continue to cook for 1 minute. Thicken the sauce with the blended cornstarch and cook another minute. Set aside.

Heat the oil in a deep-fat fryer or large wok until quite hot. Dip the slices of eggplant into the batter, let the excess batter drip off, then deep-fry. You may have to do this in several batches. Remove from the oil with a slotted spoon and drain well on paper towel.

Arrange the eggplant slices on a serving platter, pour the sauce over and serve.

Stir-Fried "Silver Sprouts"

1 ounce Chinese dried
   mushrooms
½ pound bean sprouts
½ pound pressed seasoned
   bean curd
2 ounces celery
¼ pound green peppers
2 ounces carrots
4 whole scallions
1½ teaspoons salt
¼ teaspoon freshly ground
   black pepper
1 tablespoon peanut oil
2 teaspoons chili oil
2 tablespoons rice wine or
   dry sherry
3 to 4 tablespoons water

 Serves 4

Small mung beans provide these sprouts. In Hong Kong, markets sell fresh bean sprouts plucked or trimmed at both ends. In that form they have a clean, fresh look and are ready to use, but the trimming process takes some time. They are a very nutritious addition to salads and stir-fried dishes, their mild flavor and crunchiness providing a delightful touch to every meal. When they are stir-fried with bean curd and other ingredients, as here, their color appears as a shimmering silver, hence the name of this recipe.

Try to obtain the pressed seasoned bean curd. It is cooked in a soy-flavored sauce which also imparts a pleasant brownish color to it. If unavailable, you may substitute fresh firm bean curd but you must weight it down with a heavy lid for at least 2 hours to make it even firmer and less moist. It will also have less flavor, so remember to increase your seasonings. Pan-fry the bean curd until it is firm before stir-frying, otherwise it may fall apart; this will affect the appearance but not the taste. ■

Soak the mushrooms in a large bowl of warm water for 20 minutes. Drain them and squeeze out any excess liquid. Discard the tough stalks, finely shred the caps, and put them aside.

Trim the bean sprouts. Cut the pressed bean curd, celery, peppers, carrots, and scallions into fine shreds.

Heat a wok or large frying-pan over moderate heat and add the oil. Put in the salt, pepper, and carrots and stir-fry for 1 minute. Add the celery, mushrooms, bean curd, peppers, and scallions and continue to stir-fry for 2 minutes. Stir in the rice wine and water and stir-fry until most of the liquid has evaporated. Turn onto a plate and serve at once.

Mu-shu Vegetables with Chinese Pancakes

4 eggs, beaten

4 teaspoons sesame oil

1 teaspoon salt

1 tablespoon peanut oil

½ ounce Chinese dried wood
ears (black fungus)

½ ounce Chinese lily buds

¼ pound red peppers

4 whole scallions

3 tablespoons rice wine or
dry sherry

1 tablespoon finely chopped
garlic

1 tablespoon finely chopped
fresh ginger

2 tablespoons dark soy sauce

6 ounces bean sprouts

Chinese pancakes (page 51)

Hoisin sauce, for dipping

 Serves 4

This is a vegetarian version of a traditional Chinese favorite, Mu-Shu Pork. Here, I rely upon an unusually flavorful combination of spices, vegetables, and condiments which together make one forget that pork or any other meat was ever a part of the dish. Particularly important to this recipe are the Chinese dried wood ears and lily buds. These may be difficult to obtain but are worth the extra effort of searching for them. Their textures and the flavors they absorb in the stir-frying are the basis for the success of the dish. When the combined ingredients are eaten with Chinese pancakes and hoisin sauce, what might be an ordinary dish is transformed into a festive affair. Most of the preparation may be done ahead of time and, once the pancakes are made, the rest is easily accomplished, making this a perfect dish for a dinner party. You may experiment with your own seasonal favorite vegetables or serve with rice instead of pancakes. ■

Combine the beaten eggs with 2 teaspoons of the sesame oil and salt in a small bowl. Heat a frying-pan or wok over moderate heat and add 1 tablespoon of the oil. Pour in the egg mixture and spread it quickly over the surface of the pan until it forms a thin crêpe-like pancake. There is no need to turn it over. Remove from the heat and when cool, shred the egg pancake and set aside.

Soak the dried wood ears and lily buds in warm water for about 20 minutes until soft. Meanwhile, finely shred the peppers and scallions. Squeeze the excess liquid from the black fungus and lily buds. Finely shred the wood ears, discarding the stem, and snap off the hard ends of the lily buds.

Heat a wok or large frying-pan over high heat and add the remaining peanut oil. When almost smoking, add the wood ears, lily buds, and rice wine and stir-fry for 1 minute. Add the garlic, ginger, and dark soy sauce, and stir-fry for another minute. Then put in the shredded egg, red peppers, scallions, and bean sprouts and continue to stir-fry for 3 minutes until the ingredients are thoroughly mixed. Stir in the remaining sesame oil, and turn onto a large platter. Serve with the Chinese pancakes and hoisin sauce.

Green beans in pungent sauce

1 tablespoon peanut oil
2 garlic cloves, crushed
1 tablespoon fermented chili
   bean curd
¼ teaspoon salt
1 pound Chinese long beans
   or runner beans, trimmed
   and sliced, or haricots
   verts, trimmed and left
   whole
3 tablespoons rice wine or
   dry sherry
2 tablespoons water

 Serves 2 to 4

I often enjoyed this easy-to-make dish as a child. Fresh green beans are a nutritious and inexpensive vegetable and lend themselves to spices and seasonings that complement their delicate flavor. In this recipe, the pungent spiciness of the fermented chili bean curd turns the vegetables into something quite special. You will find fermented bean curd at Asian specialty markets: you may choose from various types, ranging from mild to quite spicy, as with my favorite, chili bean curd. In using so lively a spice as chili bean curd, remember that a little goes a long way. ■

Heat a wok or large frying-pan and add the oil. When moderately hot, add the garlic, bean curd, and salt and stir-fry for about 30 seconds. Add the beans, rice wine, and water and continue to stir-fry at a moderately high heat for about 5 minutes or until the beans are thoroughly cooked, adding more water if necessary to keep the beans moist. Serve at once.

CRISPY VEGETABLE STIR-FRY

¼ pound red peppers
¼ pound green peppers
¼ pound yellow peppers
¼ pound fresh or canned
  (drained weight) water
  chestnuts
2 ounces canned bamboo
  shoots
2 teaspoons salt
3 slices of fresh ginger
2 ounces snow peas, trimmed
2 teaspoons peanut oil
3 tablespoons water

 Serves 4

I like to serve meals that appeal to the eye as well as to the palate. Therefore, when peppers are in season, I use them as often as possible: the sweetness of the reds and yellows and the mild bite of the greens delight one's senses and add a colorful dimension to any meal. Stir-frying preserves the best characteristics of peppers. When combined, as here, with the crisp texture and sweet flavor of bamboo shoots and water chestnuts and the zing of ginger, the result is a colorful, and healthy vegetable dish. Use fresh water chestnuts if possible.

Remember that the key to stir-frying vegetables is to cook the harder ones, or those with the least amount of moisture, first. ■

Cut the peppers into 1½-inch triangles. Thinly slice the water chestnuts and bamboo shoots.

Heat a wok or large frying-pan and add the oil. When moderately hot, add the salt and ginger and stir-fry for about 1 minute to allow the ginger to flavor the oil. Add the peppers and stir-fry for 2 minutes. Stir in the water chestnuts and bamboo shoots and continue to stir-fry for 2 minutes. Finally, add the snow peas and stir-fry for 30 seconds, then add the water. Stir-fry for another minute or until the snow peas are cooked, adding more water if necessary. When the vegetables are cooked serve them at once.

Stir-fried spicy carrots

1½ pounds carrots
1 tablespoon peanut oil
2 teaspoons finely chopped garlic
1 teaspoon finely chopped fresh ginger
2 dried chilies, seeded
1 tablespoon black beans, coarsely chopped
1 teaspoon sugar
2 tablespoons rice wine or dry sherry
2 teaspoons sesame oil

 Serves 4

The European carrot is now the standard in China and in Chinese cookery, although the Chinese do cultivate a larger version which is also quite sweet. Because of their distinctive taste and color, carrots combine well with other seasonings and herbs, in this case the pungent flavors of ginger, black beans, garlic, and dried chilies. The carrots are first roll-cut and then blanched. The final step of stir-frying sears the spices and allows the carrots to absorb the new flavors. These colorful and tasty carrots go well with a simple serving of plain rice or as a pleasing vegetable dish accompanying meat or poultry. They can also be served at room temperature, making them an interesting addition to any picnic menu. ■

Peel the carrots and roll-cut them according to the technique on page 42. Blanch the carrots in a large saucepan of boiling salted hot water for 4 to 5 minutes, then immerse them in cold water. Drain thoroughly.

Heat a wok or large frying-pan until moderately hot and add the oil. Put in the garlic, ginger, chilies, and black beans and stir-fry for about 1 minute. Stir in the carrots, sugar, and rice wine and continue to stir-fry for about 3 minutes or until the carrots are thoroughly heated. Add the sesame oil and continue to stir-fry for 20 seconds.

Vegetable tempura

¼ pound cauliflower
¼ pound zucchini
¼ pound carrots
¼ pound eggplant
2 ounces Chinese long beans,
    runner beans, or haricots
    verts, trimmed
1 small onion
¼ pound small whole button
    mushrooms
2 cups peanut oil

SAUCE
¼ cup dashi (page 22) or
    chicken or vegetable stock
3 tablespoons sake, rice wine,
    or dry sherry
2 tablespoons light soy sauce
1 tablespoon sugar

BATTER
1 egg, beaten
⅔ cup very cold water
½ cup all-purpose flour,
    sifted
½ teaspoon baking powder

 Serves 6–8

Of all deep-fried foods, I prefer Japanese tempura. The delicate coating of batter allows the fresh vegetable flavors to come through; there is crispness without the heaviness generally associated with batter-fried foods. The secret of tempura's lace-like quality lies in the use of a thin batter made with *very* cold or iced water mixed together just before coating the vegetables. Although tempura is commonly used with seafood such as prawns, it works as deliciously with vegetables. Cooking the tempura, by dipping the prepared vegetables in the batter and deep-frying them quickly, takes a bit of practice. The tempura must be served immediately. For an authentic Japanese taste, use dashi, an essential in Japanese cuisine in preference to stock in the dipping sauce. ∎

Cut the cauliflower into small florets about 1 to 1½ inches wide. Cut the zucchini, carrots, and eggplant into thin 4-inch long slices. Cut the beans into 4-inch pieces. Thinly slice the onion.

In a small pan, simmer the sauce ingredients together for 5 minutes. Remove the sauce from the heat, leave to cool, then pour the sauce into a small serving bowl and set aside.

Combine the batter ingredients together in a bowl and quickly strain through a fine sieve. (Do this just before you are about to deep-fry, while the oil is heating.)

Heat the oil in a deep-fat fryer or large wok until hot. Dip the vegetables in the batter and fry until golden and crispy. Remove with a slotted spoon and drain on paper towel. You will have to do this in several batches. Serve immediately with the dipping sauce.

Bitter melon with black bean sauce

1 pound bitter melon
1 tablespoon peanut oil
1½ tablespoons black beans, coarsely chopped
1 tablespoon finely chopped fresh ginger
2 teaspoons finely chopped garlic
1 tablespoon finely chopped scallions
2 teaspoons light soy sauce
1 tablespoon rice wine or dry sherry
1 teaspoon sugar
½ cup chicken or vegetable stock

 Serves 2 to 4

Bitter melon, a type of squash, is one of my favorite Chinese vegetables. True, it has a bitter quinine taste which even many Chinese do not like, but then many Westerners do not like caviar. In China, it is used in its unripe stage, when it is light green and bumpy. There are many ways to prepare it—my mother had a dozen recipes—but the most usual is to cut it up and stir-fry, as in this classic southern Chinese recipe. Look for the riper, softer, orange-colored melons, which tend to be less bitter; the blanching process also reduces the bitterness. In cooking, as often happens, the bitterness is transformed into "bite" for, while the melon brings out the best flavors of the other ingredients, they in turn seem to neutralize some of its tartness. The result is a surprisingly refreshing effect on the palate. Bitter melon is a taste worth acquiring. ■

Slice the bitter melon in half lengthways and, using a teaspoon, remove the seeds. Slice the meat widthwise into about ¼-inch pieces. Blanch the bitter melon pieces in a large saucepan of boiling water for 2 minutes. Drain, plunge them into cold water, then drain in a colander.

Heat a wok or large frying-pan and add the oil. When moderately hot, add the black beans, ginger, garlic, and scallions and stir-fry for 30 seconds. Stir in the soy sauce, rice wine, sugar, and stock. Bring the mixture to a boil and add the bitter melon. Continue to cook over high heat for about 3 minutes or until the bitter melon is completely cooked and soft. Serve at once.

CLOUD EARS STIR-FRIED WITH SNOW PEAS

½ ounce Chinese dried Cloud
  ears (black fungus)
¼ pound fresh or canned
  water chestnuts
¼ pound celery
1 tablespoon peanut oil
2 garlic cloves, crushed
½ pound snow peas, trimmed

SAUCE

1 tablespoon oyster sauce
1 teaspoon light soy sauce
2 teaspoons dark soy sauce
1 teaspoon sugar
2 teaspoons rice wine or dry
  sherry
2 teaspoons sesame oil
2 teaspoons cornstarch mixed
  with 2 teaspoons water
⅔ cup chicken or vegetable
  stock

 Serves 4

This is a colorful and wholesome vegetable dish that is easily assembled for a family dinner. It is a classic combination of the tastes and textures so typical of Chinese cooking. The cloud ears have little flavor of their own but, like mushrooms in general, they readily absorb other flavors and retain their chewy texture. And, like truffles in French cuisine, cloud ears enhance an entire recipe, bringing out the best in the foods. ■

Soak the cloud ears in warm water for 20 minutes until soft. Set aside.

If you are using fresh water chestnuts, peel them. If you are using canned water chestnuts, drain them well and rinse in cold water. Thinly slice the water chestnuts. String the celery and slice diagonally.

Heat a wok or large frying-pan over a medium heat and add the oil. When hot, add the garlic and stir-fry for 30 seconds. Then add the cloud ears and celery and stir-fry for 2 minutes. Stir in the snow peas and fresh water chestnuts and stir-fry another minute. Add all the sauce ingredients, except for the blended cornstarch. Bring the sauce to a boil and stir in the cornstarch mixture. If you are using canned water chestnuts, add now and warm through. Turn the mixture onto a serving platter and serve at once.

Stir-Fried Lettuce

1 pound iceberg or romaine
   lettuce
1 tablespoon peanut oil
2 garlic cloves, crushed
1 teaspoon finely chopped
   fresh ginger
3 tablespoons chicken or
   vegetable stock
1 tablespoon light soy sauce
¼ teaspoon salt
1 teaspoon sugar
½ teaspoon cornstarch mixed
   with 1 teaspoon water

 Serves 2 to 4

Lettuce is used so often in the West as a garnish and salad that one tends to forget it is a vegetable and, as such, capable of a greater culinary role. As a child at home, I ate only cooked lettuce, and I was a bit put off to see my Western friends eating it raw in their lunch sandwiches. In Hong Kong, the street-side food vendors or food stalls offer stir-fried lettuce as a vegetable dish to accompany rice and chicken dishes. It works very well, provided you use firm lettuce and stir-fry it very quickly. ■

Separate the lettuce leaves and wash well. Cut the large leaves in half.

   Heat a wok or large frying-pan and add the oil. When moderately hot, add the garlic and ginger and stir-fry for 30 seconds. Next, add the lettuce and stir-fry quickly for a few seconds. Stir in the rest of the ingredients except the cornstarch mixture. Give a couple of stirs and then remove the lettuce to a platter with a slotted spoon. Add the blended cornstarch to the sauce and bring to a boil. When the sauce thickens, pour over the lettuce and serve at once.

Braised chinese mushrooms

¼ pound Chinese dried
   mushrooms
1 tablespoon peanut oil

SAUCE

1¼ cups chicken or vegetable
   stock
2 tablespoons dark soy sauce
2 tablespoons sugar
2 teaspoons sesame oil
1 tablespoon rice wine or dry
   sherry

GARNISH

2 scallions, sliced

 Serves 4

Chinese family banquets, held on special occasions, are truly feasts. As a boy attending such gala affairs, I always looked for the large plate of beautifully arranged, thick Chinese mushrooms that traditionally graced the table. Braised in a rich sauce, smoky in taste, chewy in texture, these mushrooms were favorites of mine. I ate them whenever I could, as any Western youth might eat potato chips or roasted peanuts. The large dried variety of Chinese mushrooms recommended for this recipe can be expensive, but they are well worth it for a special occasion. Do not cut up the caps, as left whole, they absorb the sauce better. The dish reheats beautifully, which makes it ideal for a large dinner party since it can be prepared in advance. ■

Soak the dried mushrooms in warm water for 20 minutes until soft. Squeeze the excess liquid from the mushrooms and remove and discard the stalks. Leave the mushrooms whole.

Heat a wok or large frying-pan and add the oil. Put in the mushrooms and stir-fry for a few seconds. Quickly add the sauce ingredients and turn the heat down. Braise the mushrooms for 7 minutes, stirring continually, until the mushrooms have absorbed most of the sauce. Turn the mixture onto a serving platter and garnish with the scallions.

CLOUD EARS IN HOISIN SAUCE

1 ounce Chinese dried cloud
ears (black fungus)
1 tablespoon peanut oil
2 garlic cloves, crushed
¼ teaspoon salt
3 tablespoons rice wine or
dry sherry
1¼ cups chicken or vegetable
stock
1 tablespoon light soy sauce
3 tablespoons hoisin sauce
2 teaspoons sesame oil
1 teaspoon cornstarch mixed
with 1 teaspoon water

 Serves 4

In this recipe, cloud ears are stir-fried in the strongly flavored hoisin sauce, which is absorbed thoroughly while the cloud ears still retain their chewy texture. If you wish, you may add another vegetable such as cauliflower or broccoli; but by themselves the cloud ears, given zest by the rich sauce, work very well as a vegetable dish for any meal. ∎

Soak the dried cloud ears in warm water for 20 minutes until soft. Rinse in cold water and drain in a colander.

Heat a wok or frying-pan until hot and add the oil and garlic. Stir-fry for 30 seconds, then add the cloud ears. Continue to stir-fry for another 2 minutes. Stir in the rest of the ingredients, except for the cornstarch mixture. Continue to cook for another 2 minutes, add the blended cornstarch and when the sauce thickens, the dish is ready to be served.

GRILLED MUSHROOMS WITH LEMON SAUCE

1 pound large button
   mushrooms
2 teaspoons salt

SAUCE

2 tablespoons lemon juice
1 tablespoon dark soy sauce
1 tablespoon sake, rice wine
   or dry sherry
2 teaspoons sugar
2 tablespoons finely chopped
   scallions

 Serves 4

This recipe is of Japanese origin, simple but unusual and quite delicious. It offers a different way to enjoy fresh mushrooms and is a perfect side dish to enliven a barbecue or as an accompaniment to grilled meats or poultry. The mushrooms may also be cooked using your oven broiler, so the dish may be savored indoors during the winter as well, missing only the smoky barbecue flavor. For an authentic taste, try to obtain Japanese sake for the sauce; if it cannot be had, rice wine or dry sherry are acceptable substitutes. The lemon sauce may be made beforehand. ▪

Sprinkle the mushrooms with the salt and mix well. Put the mushrooms into a colander and let drain for 20 minutes. When the mushrooms have drained, rinse them in water and blot dry with paper towel.

Heat the sauce ingredients together in a small saucepan until the sugar dissolves. Let cool.

Soak some wooden skewers in cold water for 5 minutes. Thread 3 or 4 mushrooms on each skewer and cook under a broiler or on a barbecue. When they are cooked, remove from the skewers, mix them with the sauce and serve.

Button mushrooms in oyster sauce

2 teaspoons peanut oil
2 garlic cloves, crushed
1 pound small whole button
  mushrooms
1 tablespoon dark soy sauce
1 tablespoon oyster sauce
1 teaspoon sugar
2 tablespoons rice wine or
  dry sherry

 *Serves 2 to 4*

Button mushrooms are unknown in the East, but I have found that they, like all good edible fungi, are perfectly amenable to Chinese and other Asian spices and seasonings. Here I have combined them with a classic southern Chinese flavor of oyster sauce. ▪

Heat a wok or large frying-pan and add the oil. Put in the garlic and stir-fry for 30 seconds. Add the mushrooms and stir-fry for 1 minute. Stir in the soy sauce, oyster sauce, sugar, and rice wine. Turn the heat down and simmer slowly for 5 minutes, stirring from time to time. When the mushrooms are cooked, turn the heat back to high and continue stirring until most of the liquid has evaporated and the dish is ready to be served.

STIR-FRIED CUCUMBERS

1½ pounds cucumbers
2¼ teaspoons salt
1 tablespoon peanut oil
2 tablespoons dark soy sauce
1 tablespoon rice wine or dry
   sherry
2 teaspoons sesame oil
1 teaspoon chili oil

 Serves 4

Cucumbers are too often taken for granted, their cool unobtrusive virtues having rendered them less interesting than other vegetables and fit only for salad. Stir-fried, however, they take on an unexpected boldness. My uncle used to cook them with little pieces of pork, but I have learned that they are tasty all by themselves with a complementary sauce. Salt the cucumbers first to rid them of their excess liquid. Stir-fried and made savory by the sauce, the cucumbers make a wonderful vegetable side dish that is ideal for lunch or dinner. ■

Peel the cucumbers, slice them in half lengthways, and using a teaspoon, remove the seeds. Cut the cucumber halves into 3-inch pieces. Sprinkle them with 2 teaspoons of the salt and mix well. Put the salted cucumbers into a colander and let them sit for 20 minutes to drain. This rids the cucumbers of any excess liquid. When the cucumber pieces have drained, rinse in water and blot dry with paper towel.

Heat a wok or large frying-pan until hot and add the oil. Put in the cucumber and stir-fry for 2 minutes. Stir in the remaining salt, soy sauce, and rice wine and continue to stir-fry for another 2 minutes. Add the sesame and chili oil and give the mixture several good stirs. Serve at once.

Vegetable medley with tomato-garlic sauce

¼ pound Chinese long beans, runner beans, or haricot vert, trimmed
¼ pound zucchini
¼ pound cauliflower
¼ pound broccoli
¼ pound carrots
¼ pound snow peas, trimmed
1 tablespoon peanut oil

SAUCE

2 tablespoons finely chopped garlic
3 tablespoons finely chopped shallots
1 teaspoon seeded and finely chopped dried chilies
¾ pound fresh or canned tomatoes
1 tablespoon fish sauce

GARNISH

1 tablespoon finely chopped fresh coriander

 Serves 4 to 6

In Asian cooking, the preference is often for dipping sauces rather than for sauces that cover the food on the plate. In this recipe from Vietnam, each type of vegetable is blanched individually, thus making allowance for the different cooking requirements of each vegetable. Remember to plunge them immediately into cold water to prevent further cooking. The dipping sauce is quite lively, which is exactly what the plain, sweet, cool vegetables need. This is a dish ideal for a buffet and cocktails. ■

Cut the beans into 3-inch lengths. Cut the zucchini into 3-inch long by ½-inch wide pieces. Cut the cauliflower into small florets about 1 to 1½-inches wide. Cut off the broccoli head and break it into small florets. Peel and thinly slice the broccoli stalks. Peel and cut the carrots into 3-inch long by ½-inch wide pieces.

Blanch each of the vegetables separately in a large saucepan of boiling salted water: 1 minute for the snow peas, 2 minutes for the beans and zucchini, 4 minutes for the cauliflower, broccoli and carrots. As you take out each vegetable, plunge it into cold water until cooled, then drain well.

For the sauce, if you are using fresh tomatoes, peel, seed and cut into 1-inch cubes. If you are using canned tomatoes, chop them into small chunks. Combine the tomatoes with the rest of the sauce ingredients and purée the mixture in blender or food processor. Arrange the vegetables on a serving platter together with the dipping sauce in a separate bowl. Garnish the sauce with the fresh coriander. Serve immediately or refrigerate and serve later.

Vietnamese-style Vegetables

½ pound firm bean curd

1¼ cups peanut oil, for deep-frying

¼ pound cauliflower

1½ tablespoons peanut oil

2 garlic cloves, crushed

2 tablespoons finely chopped shallots

½ pound small button mushrooms

½ teaspoon salt

⅔ cup water

1 tablespoon light soy sauce

2 teaspoons fish sauce

3 tablespoons finely chopped fresh coriander

Serves 4

This is a home-style family dish that is also served in Vietnamese restaurants. Its main ingredients are nutritious bean curd and mushrooms, combined with cauliflower, which provides a new texture and flavor, and with a spicy fish sauce to enliven the dish. The bean curd, cut into thin strips and deep-fried, does not break up when stir-fried. Serve this substantial dish with plain rice and you have a complete meal. ■

Cut the bean curd into 3-inch long by ½-inch thick strips.

Heat the 1¼ cup oil in a deep-fat fryer or a large wok until it almost smokes. Deep-fry the bean curd strips in 2 batches. When each batch is light brown, remove and drain well on paper towel.

Cut the cauliflower into small florets about 1 to 1½ inches wide. Blanch the florets in a large saucepan of boiling salted water for several minutes, then immerse in cold water and drain thoroughly.

Heat a wok or large frying-pan and add the 1½ tablespoons oil. Put in the garlic and shallots and stir-fry for 30 seconds. Then add the mushrooms, salt, water, soy sauce, and fish sauce and stir-fry for 5 minutes. Gently stir in the bean curd, cauliflower, and fresh coriander and continue to stir-fry for 2 minutes or until the cauliflower and bean curd are heated through. It is then ready to be served.

Eggs with chinese mushrooms

1 ounce Chinese dried
  mushrooms
½ ounce Chinese dried cloud
  ears (black fungus)
½ pound yellow onions
4 eggs, beaten
2½ teaspoons salt
1 tablespoon sesame oil
1 tablespoon peanut oil
2 tablespoons rice wine or
  dried sherry
1 tablespoon light soy
3 tablespoons chicken or
  vegetable stock

GARNISH

3 tablespoons chopped
  scallions
1 teaspoon sesame oil

 Serves 4

Eggs are popular in Eastern vegetarian cookery. In China, the tradition is always to contrast the softness of the eggs with firm, crunchy, or crisp textures. In this recipe, I combine two varieties of dried firm mushrooms, one of them cloud ears, with eggs. Do try to obtain the Chinese dried variety. You may substitute fresh button mushrooms, but be sure to cook them until most of the moisture has gone. This is an easy-to-prepare dish and goes wonderfully with rice or as a filling for Chinese Pancakes (page 51). ∎

Soak the Chinese dried mushrooms and cloud ears in separate bowls of warm water for about 20 minutes, then drain. Rinse the cloud ears well and leave whole. Squeeze out any excess liquid from the dried mushrooms, discard the tough stalks, then shred the caps and put them aside. Finely slice the onions. Combine the eggs with 2 teaspoons of the salt and sesame oil in a small bowl.

Heat a wok or large frying-pan over high heat and add 1 tablespoon of the oil. Put in the onions and stir-fry for 4 minutes until soft and translucent. Remove them and wipe the wok clean. Reheat the wok over high heat and add the remaining oil. Add the mushrooms, cloud ears, rice wine, soy sauce, and remaining salt and stir-fry for 2 minutes. Stir in the stock and return the cooked onions to the wok. Continue to stir-fry for 1 minute. Then add the egg mixture and stir several times. The dish is ready when the eggs have set. Transfer to a platter and garnish with the scallions and sesame oil.

CRISPY SCALLION OMELETTE

6 scallions
½ ounce fresh chili
6 eggs, beaten
1 tablespoon sesame oil
3 tablespoons finely chopped
  scallions
½ teaspoon salt
2 teaspoons light soy sauce
4 tablespoons peanut oil

GARNISH
1 tablespoon finely chopped
  fresh coriander

 Serves 2

Here the mildness and soft texture of the eggs are transformed by the cooking process and the addition of other textures and seasonings. My mother often prepared just such a dish when she was in a hurry as it was quick and economical. We would have it over rice, with a touch of oyster sauce. ■

Cut the scallions diagonally into 2-inch lengths. Finely shred the chili. In a large bowl, mix the eggs, sesame oil, finely chopped scallions, salt, and light soy.

Heat a wok or large frying-pan over high heat and add 1 tablespoon of the oil. Put in the scallion pieces and the chili and stir-fry them for 2 minutes. Remove them and wipe the wok clean. Reheat the wok and add 3 tablespoons of oil and, when hot, add the egg mixture. When the egg begins to cook, return the cooked scallions and chili to the wok and continue to cook over high heat for 2 minutes until brown and crispy. Flip the omelette over and brown the other side. Remove it to a platter and garnish with the coriander. Serve at once.

Bean Curd Dishes

Of all the vegetarian foods, bean curd (page 16) is the most versatile and important in Asian cooking. High in protein but low in cholesterol, plain but absorbent, soft-textured but strong, it is nutritious and receptive to all types of cooking. Bean curd can be boiled, simmered, steamed, braised, deep-fried, pan-fried or used as a filling. Adding substance without an intrusive taste, it combines well with all foods. Moreover, it is quite inexpensive. In fact, bean curd represents such a good buy that the slang expression in eastern Chinese dialects for easily taking advantage of a person is "eating bean curd." It is known as doufu in Chinese or tofu in Japanese.

The many techniques and combinations for cooking bean curd are represented in this chapter. It can be simply simmered, as in Bean Curd Custard in Oyster Sauce or deep-fried as in Crispy Bean Curd Cubes with Peanut Dipping Sauce, or braised in a Southeast Asian-style sauce as in Coconut-Stewed Bean Curd and Vegetables. Tasting bean curd in so many different forms will persuade even the most skeptical of its wonderful properties.

SWEET AND SOUR BEAN CURD

1 pound firm bean curd
1¼ cups peanut oil, for deep-
    frying
2 ounces carrots
2 ounces red peppers
1 pound fresh pineapple or
    10 ounces canned
    pineapple

SAUCE

2 garlic cloves, crushed
2 tablespoons tomato paste
1 tablespoon finely chopped
    lemongrass (optional)
1 tablespoon white rice
    vinegar or cider vinegar
2 tablespoons rice wine or
    dry sherry
1 tablespoon light soy sauce
1 tablespoon sugar
⅔ cup chicken or vegetable
    stock
2 teaspoons cornstarch mixed
    with 2 teaspoons water

GARNISH

fresh coriander leaves

Serves 2 to 4

Sweet and sour sauces must never be too sweet or too vinegary. When properly made they are a delight. As the contrasting tastes alternate and combine on the palate, one understands why well-prepared sweet and sour dishes are justly praised classics. Such a sauce lends itself to many different types of food but combines particularly well with bean curd. Here the bean curd is deep-fried, giving it an interesting spongy texture and enhancing its absorbent nature. The sweet pineapple both balances and emphasizes the rich, tangy, sour sharpness of the sauce, all combining to form the essence of sweet and sour. This unusual nutritious dish reheats well and may be made in advance. Serve it with rice and you have a complete meal. ■

Cut the bean curd into 1-inch cubes. Heat the oil in a deep-fat fryer or large wok. When the oil is almost smoking, deep-fry the bean curd cubes. You may have to do this in several batches. Drain on paper towel and set aside.

Cut the carrots into 1-inch rounds and blanch in a small sauce-pan of boiling water for 3 minutes. Drain and set aside. Cut the pepper into 1-inch squares. Peel, core, and slice the pineapple, and cut into 1-inch cubes.

Combine the sauce ingredients together in a large saucepan and bring to a boil. Add the carrot and red pepper and stir well. Stir the blended cornstarch into the sauce and bring it back to a boil. Reduce the heat to a simmering point and gently put in the bean curd and the pineapple. Mix well, then turn the mixture onto a deep platter. Garnish and serve at once.

Savory bean curd casserole

1 ounce Chinese dried
  mushrooms
¾ pound Chinese cabbage or
  white cabbage
1 pound firm bean curd
2 cups peanut oil, for deep-
  frying
1 tablespoon peanut oil
2 tablespoons fermented red
  bean curd
1 tablespoon finely chopped
  fresh ginger
1½ tablespoons finely
  chopped garlic
2 ounces bean thread
  (transparent) noodles
1 teaspoon salt
2 teaspoons sugar
3 tablespoons rice wine or
  dry sherry
1 tablespoon light soy sauce
3 tablespoons scallions
1¼ cups chicken or vegetable
  stock

 Serves 4

There are many different variations of bean curd, and one of the tastiest is fermented red bean curd. This impressive condiment is preserved by fermentation in a solution of red rice, salt, and spices. It has a pungent aroma which dissipates as it cooks, leaving a flavor and fragrance that richly complements a stew or casserole, especially one made with bean curd. The other spices combine perfectly with the fermented bean curd and create a sauce that permeates the bean thread noodles as well. My mother often made a version of this casserole during the cold Chicago winters of my childhood. Its rich aromas and combination of flavors evoke memories of those days. This is a hearty dish that reheats easily and is perfect over rice. ■

Soak the dried mushrooms in warm water for about 20 minutes until they are soft. Squeeze the excess liquid from the mushrooms, and remove and discard their stalks. Shred the Chinese cabbage.

Cut the bean curd into 1-inch cubes. Heat the oil in a deep-fat fryer or large wok. When the oil is almost smoking, deep-fry the bean curd cubes. You may have to do this in several batches. Remove and drain on paper towel.

Heat a wok or large frying-pan and add 1 tablespoon oil. Put in the fermented bean curd, ginger, and garlic, and stir-fry for about 30 seconds. Add the rest of the ingredients. Bring the mixture to a simmer and add the deep-fried bean curd. Cover tightly and braise gently for about 20 minutes.

To reheat, bring to a simmer on low heat until the mixture is hot.

Stuffed bean curd squares

1 pound firm bean curd
3 tablespoons peanut oil

FILLING

½ ounce Chinese dried
   mushrooms
1 teaspoon finely chopped
   scallions
½ teaspoon finely chopped
   fresh ginger
3 tablespoons roasted
   peanuts, coarsely chopped
½ teaspoon salt
½ teaspoon pepper
1 tablespoon peanut oil
1 teaspoon sugar
1 teaspoon yellow bean sauce
2 tablespoons coarsely
   chopped garlic
½ teaspoon Sichuan
   peppercorns, roasted and
   ground (page 31)

Serves 2 to 4

Bean curd suffers from an undeserved reputation for excessive bland-
ness and dullness. Part of the problem lies in the way it is generally
prepared in the West. One authority writes: "The West has picked up
the idea and developed it much further, climaxing in the production
of textured vegetable protein (TVP), but has—characteristically—ig-
nored the problem of making the result taste good. The ideal in the
West seems to be to make it tasteless." Bean curd is bland and so is
rice, but this is a virtue when properly approached. The trick is to
take advantage of bean curd's generous receptivity to other foods, spices,
and seasonings. In this recipe, which my cooking colleague, Gordon
Wing, helped to create, we stuffed the bean curd with a mixture of
ginger, mushrooms, onions, and other flavors and textures, then pan-
fried and covered the bean curd squares with a savory sauce.

    Serve with rice. ■

Soak the dried mushrooms in a bowl of warm water for 20 minutes.
Drain them, and squeeze out any excess liquid. Cut off and discard
the stalks and coarsely chop the mushroom caps.

    Cut the bean curd into 4 pieces to make squares. With a tea-
spoon, scoop out 1 tablespoon of bean curd from the top, without
breaking through to the bottom. You will now have a square of bean
curd with a dip in the center of the top. This is where the filling
will go.

    Heat a wok or frying-pan over moderate heat and add one table-
spoon of oil. Put in the filling ingredients and stir-fry for 2 minutes.
Let the mixture cool, then finely chop in a blender. Gently spoon the

1 tablespoon oyster sauce

1 tablespoon light soy sauce

1 tablespoon rice wine or dry
   sherry

½ teaspoon cornstarch mixed
   with 3 tablespoons water

filling into the hollowed-out bean curd squares.

Heat a frying-pan or wok over high heat and add 2 tablespoons of oil. When hot, add the stuffed bean curd squares, unfilled side down. Lower the heat and fry, turning them over from time to time until they are brown all over. You may have to do this in 2 batches, adding more oil if necessary. Remove the stuffed bean curd, drain on paper towel, and arrange on a platter.

Meanwhile, wipe out the wok and bring the sauce ingredients to a simmer. Pour this mixture over the bean curd and serve at once.

Bean curd custard in oyster sauce

1 pound soft bean curd

1 tablespoon peanut oil

2 slices fresh ginger

2½ tablespoons oyster sauce

1 teaspoon light soy sauce

1 tablespoon rice wine or dry
   sherry

⅔ cup chicken or vegetable
   stock

1 teaspoon sugar

1 teaspoon cornstarch mixed
   with 1 teaspoon water

 Serves 2 to 4

For a high-protein, vegetarian main dish, try this simple recipe. Served with fresh vegetables and plain rice, you have a wholesome family meal. The soft bean curd must be handled more gently than the firm variety, but it will be like eating a wonderful silky savory custard. Always use the freshest bean curd available. ▪

Cut the bean curd into 1½-inch cubes.

Heat the oil in a wok or large frying-pan and add the oil. When moderately hot, add the ginger slices, oyster sauce, soy sauce, rice wine, stock, and sugar and stir for 1 minute, then add the blended cornstarch. When the mixture begins to thicken, add the bean curd and simmer gently to heat through. Serve at once.

GRILLED BEAN CURD SHISH KEBABS

1 pound firm bean curd

MARINADE

3 tablespoons light soy sauce
1 tablespoon sesame paste or
   peanut butter
1 tablespoon chili bean sauce
1 tablespoon Chinese white
   rice vinegar or cider
   vinegar
1 tablespoon rice wine or dry
   sherry

 *Serves 2 to 4*

In this recipe, bean curd readily absorbs the marinade and then grills perfectly. This is really an East-West combination, inspired by a wonderful vegetarian restaurant in San Francisco called "Greens." Always buy the freshest bean curd. For this recipe, you will need the firm variety, as soft bean curd is not suitable for skewering. You can add other vegetables, such as small tomatoes, peppers, and onions to make real shish kebabs. This is an excellent side dish or makes a perfect accompaniment to drinks. ▪

Place the bean curd between several layers of paper towel with a heavy weight on top, such as a heavy lid. Let the bean curd sit for 1 hour.

Mix all the marinade ingredients together in a small bowl. Cut the bean curd into 2-inch cubes and add to the marinade. Marinate the cubes for 1 hour, or longer for a stronger flavor, turning them at least once.

Meanwhile, soak some wooden skewers in cold water for 5 minutes. Thread the bean curd cubes on the skewers, taking care to put no more than 3 to 4 on each skewer. Cook the bean curd cubes under the broiler or on a barbecue, 2 to 3 minutes on each side or until brown, basting once with the marinade.

Serve them with your choice of dipping sauces (page 19).

Home-style spicy bean curd

1 pound soft bean curd,
  drained
1 tablespoon peanut oil
1 tablespoon finely chopped
  fresh ginger
1 tablespoon finely chopped
  garlic
1 tablespoon chili bean sauce
1 teaspoon yellow bean sauce
2 teaspoons sugar
¼ cup chicken or vegetable
  stock
2 tablespoons rice wine or
  dry sherry
1 teaspoon cornstarch mixed
  with 1 teaspoon water

GARNISH

2 teaspoons sesame oil
2 tablespoons finely chopped
  scallions

 Serves 2 to 4

This recipe is my adaptation of "Ma Po's home-cooked bean curd," a popular and traditional Sichuan dish I first experienced in a Sichuan-style restaurant in Hong Kong. The Sichuan style emphasizes hot spices and strong seasonings with which bean curd readily combines. I have made this into a vegetarian dish by omitting the minced beef or pork that is normally used. Bean curd is such a good protein and the sauce and garnish are so full of flavor that the meat is not missed, either nutritionally or as a flavor. Note that here I use *soft* bean curd, so that the result is a spicy and savory custard-like dish, perfect with rice, crispy noodles, or bread. ▪

Cut the bean curd into 1-inch cubes and set aside. Heat a wok or large frying-pan over high heat and add the oil. Put in the ginger, garlic, chili bean sauce, and bean sauce and stir-fry for 30 seconds. Add the sugar, stock, and rice wine and cook for 2 minutes. Stir the blended cornstarch into the wok. When the sauce has slightly thickened, add the bean curd cubes and stir gently. Continue to cook for 2 minutes until the bean curd is heated through. Garnish and serve at once.

Simple bean curd and mushroom stir-fry

1 pound firm bean curd
4 tablespoons peanut oil
½ pound small whole button
    mushrooms
2 cloves garlic, crushed
¼ teaspoon salt

SAUCE

1 tablespoon dark soy sauce
2 tablespoons rice wine or
    dry sherry
2 teaspoons sugar
2 tablespoons chicken or
    vegetable stock

GARNISH

2 scallions, sliced on the
    diagonal

 Serves 2 to 4

In this healthy family dish, the lightly fried bean curd with a slightly crispy surface sets off the texture of the braised mushrooms perfectly. Remember to fry the delicate bean curd squares gently. This dish reheats well and is even better the second day, although of course some of the crispness will be gone. ■

Cut the bean curd into 2-inch by ½-inch squares.

Heat a wok or large frying-pan and add 3 tablespoons of the oil. When the oil is hot, fry the bean curd on each side until golden brown. You may have to do this in several batches. Drain each cooked batch on paper towel.

Drain the oil and wipe the wok clean. Reheat the wok over moderate heat and add the remaining tablespoon of oil. Put in the garlic and salt and stir-fry for 30 seconds. Stir in the mushrooms and the sauce ingredients. Cook over moderate heat for 5 minutes or until the mushrooms are cooked. Return the bean curd to the wok and, once it is heated through, garnish and serve.

Pan-fried bean curd with leeks

1 pound firm bean curd
3 tablespoons peanut oil
¾ pound leeks
3 cloves garlic, crushed
1 dried chili, seeded
2 teaspoons chili bean sauce
1½ tablespoons dark soy
    sauce
2 teaspoons sugar
1 tablespoon rice wine or dry
    sherry
⅔ cup chicken or vegetable
    stock

 *Serves 2 to 4*

Leeks are popular throughout China but especially in the north, where this recipe came from. They are an ideal accompaniment to bean curd because of their texture and robust flavor. This is good, simple fare of the kind Chinese families enjoy at home. Serve with plain rice. ■

Cut the bean curd in half, then cut again on the diagonal into triangles. Heat a wok or large frying-pan over moderate heat and add the oil. Fry the bean curd triangles until they are golden brown. You may have to do this in several batches. Drain them on paper towel.

Cut the leeks into shreds, discarding the green parts. Wash well; you may have to do this several times.

Reheat the wok over high heat. Put in the garlic and chili and stir-fry for 30 seconds. Add the leeks and continue to stir-fry for 3 minutes, then add the rest of the ingredients. Bring the mixture to a boil. Turn the heat down to a simmer and return the bean curd triangles to the mixture. Cook for another 3 minutes or until the bean curd is heated through. Serve at once.

CANTONESE-STYLE BEAN CURD WITH CHINESE GREENS

1 pound firm bean curd
1 pound Chinese greens
1¼ cups peanut oil for deep-
frying
1 tablespoon peanut oil
4 garlic cloves, crushed
3 tablespoons oyster sauce
⅔ cup chicken or vegetable
stock
1 tablespoon cornstarch
mixed with 1 tablespoon
water

Serves 2 to 4

This tasty dish is a staple item on the food stalls and in the kitchens of Hong Kong. It is nutritious, inexpensive, and substantial. Chinese greens have a light, earthy, fresh taste and go well with bean curd. Caramel-colored oyster sauce is a savory blend of oysters and selected spices with a meaty aroma. This is an easy-to-make treat, and when served with plain rice makes a full meal. You may substitute Swiss chard or spinach for the Chinese greens. ∎

Cut the bean curd into 1-inch cubes. Cut the Chinese greens into 3-inch pieces.

Heat the 1¼ cups oil in a deep-fat fryer or large wok until it almost smokes. Deep-fry the bean curd cubes in several batches. When each batch of bean curd cubes is lightly browned, about 1 to 2 minutes, remove and drain well on paper towel.

Heat a wok or large frying-pan and add 1 tablespoon of oil. When hot, put in the garlic and Chinese greens and stir-fry for 2 minutes over high heat. Stir in the oyster sauce, stock, and blended cornstarch. Reduce the heat to very low and add the bean curd cubes. Simmer for 3 minutes or until the bean curd is heated through.

CRISPY BEAN CURD CUBES WITH PEANUT DIPPING SAUCE

¾ pound firm bean curd cut
    into 1-inch cubes
1¼ cups peanut oil, for deep-
    frying

SAUCE

1 ounce roasted peanuts
1 tablespoon sugar
2 tablespoons water
2 teaspoons Chinese white
    rice vinegar or cider
    vinegar
1 tablespoon finely chopped
    fresh coriander
½ teaspoon salt
½ teaspoon chili oil

 Serves 4 to 6

In this delectable recipe, based on a dish I once enjoyed in Thailand, the peanut dipping sauce provides the zest and color for the bean curd. In Thailand, roasted peanuts are pounded into a paste which is much easier to use than our peanut butter; some little bits of peanut are left in the paste to provide a crunchy texture. Here, the fried cubes of bean curd, crusty on the outside and spongy soft inside, are dipped into the sauce, making a delightful appetizer or cocktail food. Serve the bean curd hot as its skin toughens when it cools. ∎

Cut the bean curd into 1-inch cubes.

    Combine the sauce ingredients together in a small bowl and set aside.

    Heat the 1¼ cups oil in a deep-fat fryer or a large wok until it almost smokes. Deep-fry the bean curd cubes in two batches. When each batch of bean curd cubes is lightly browned, remove and drain well on paper towel.

    Arrange the bean curd cubes on a platter and serve the peanut sauce separately as a dipping sauce.

COCONUT-STEWED BEAN CURD AND VEGETABLES

1 pound firm bean curd
½ pound cauliflower
¼ pound Chinese long beans,
  runner beans, or French
  haricots verts
¼ pound carrots
¼ pound fresh or frozen peas
1⅓ cups peanut oil, for deep-
  frying
2 cups fresh or canned
  coconut milk (page 20)
⅔ cup water
½ teaspoon salt
2 tablespoons dark soy sauce
2 teaspoons sugar
1 tablespoon fish sauce

 Serves 4

Vegetable stews enjoy an honorable place in the Chinese cuisine and are popular throughout Southeast Asia. Meat and poultry are often expensive, but the cheaper bean curd and vegetables provide a healthful and tasty—and in many ways even superior—substitute. They are the principal dishes today for most rural Indonesian families and, in Thailand, they are prominent among the non-curry meals available at food stalls. This recipe is of Vietnamese origin. The bean curd is deep-fried and then braised with vegetables in a rich coconut milk broth flavored with fish sauce. You may substitute other vegetables, such as Brussels sprouts, turnips, or parsnips if you like—always use those that are in season. As with stews in general, vegetable stews can be made well in advance, and they taste better the day after preparation—but reheat them slowly. Serve with plain rice. ■

Cut the bean curd into 1-inch cubes. Cut the cauliflower into small florets about 1 to 1½ inches wide. Slice the beans into 3-inch pieces. Peel and cut the carrots into ½-inch cubes. If you are using fresh peas, blanch them for 3 minutes in a saucepan of boiling water, then drain them in a colander. (There is no need to blanch the frozen peas.)

Heat the 1¼ cups oil in a deep-fat fryer or a large wok until it almost smokes. Deep-fry the bean curd cubes for 1 to 2 minutes in two batches. When each batch of bean curd cubes is lightly browned, remove and drain well on paper towel.

Bring the coconut milk, water, dark soy, sugar, and fish sauce to a boil in a large saucepan. Reduce the heat to a simmer, add the vegetables and the bean curd, cover tightly, and braise for about 20 minutes or until the vegetables are cooked.

RED-COOKED BEAN CURD

1 pound firm bean curd
3 tablespoons peanut oil

SAUCE

2 tablespoons dark soy sauce
1 tablespoon rice wine or dry
   sherry
2 tablespoons hoisin sauce
½ teaspoon Sichuan
   peppercorns, roasted and
   finely ground (page 31)
1 teaspoon chili bean sauce
1 teaspoon sugar
2 teaspoons finely chopped
   fresh ginger
¼ teaspoon salt
⅔ cup chicken or vegetable
   stock
1 tablespoon peanut oil

 Serves 2 to 4

"Red-cooked" is a term applied to Chinese dishes braised and spiced with the robust, dark, brownish-red seasoning of hoisin sauce, made from soybean flour, red beans, chilies, sugar, salt, garlic, and spices. The fried bean curd has a crispy surface texture while its soft interior readily absorbs the sauce. This is a flavorful dish that is a complete meal with other vegetable or meat dishes and plain rice. ▪

Cut the bean curd into 1-inch cubes. Heat a wok or large frying-pan and add the oil. When moderately hot, add the bean curd and fry for 1 to 2 minutes until golden brown. Set aside. Wipe the wok clean.

Add all the sauce ingredients to the wok and bring to a slow simmer. Return the bean curd to the wok and simmer gently in this mixture for about 5 minutes. Turn out onto a serving platter and serve at once.

Hot Pasta & Noodles

Pasta or noodles come in many forms in China, Japan, and Southeast Asia. I need only name the various types of Japanese pasta to illustrate: harusame, hiyamugi, kishimen, maifun, ramen, shiratake, soba, somen, udon. These are made from wheat, rice, buckwheat, bean threads, and yam threads. Throughout Asia, pasta is eaten in the form of noodles, wontons, and pasta wrappers. These foods have been a part of the diet of this region for many hundreds of years.

All pasta is characterized by subtle variations of texture and color, absorbent receptivity to sauces, and congeniality to other foods, plus excellent nutritional values. Its universal popularity is therefore not surprising.

The word "pasta" is, of course, an Italian word. I use it because it has entered our language as a generic term meaning unleavened dough, rolled out and formed into different shapes. One regional difference is that some Asian pastas are made from rice flour rather than wheat.

In this book, I have combined various pastas with spices and flavors typical of China, Japan, and Southeast Asia. I have included as well some East-West blends. The dishes are wholesome, sustaining, light, and relatively easy to make. They may serve as appetizers, side dishes or complete meals in themselves. Make and savor them, and they will immediately become a regular part of your diet.

Although there are many types of pasta noodles found in Asia, not all of them are available here in the West. Therefore I have restricted myself to those which are dried and can be found in supermarkets or Asian specialty markets. Some may not be found at supermarkets but are easily obtained by mail order. Below are some of the most common types of noodles available.

□ WHEAT NOODLES AND EGG NOODLES

These are made from hard or soft wheat flour and water. If egg has been added, the noodles are usually labelled as egg noodles. They can be bought dried or fresh from Asian specialty markets, and many supermarkets and delicatessens also stock the dried variety. Flat noodles are usually used in soups, and rounded noodles are best for stir-frying. If you can't get Chinese noodles, you can use Italian egg noodles (dried or fresh) instead.

To cook wheat and egg noodles

Noodles are very good boiled and served instead of plain rice with main dishes. I think dried wheat or fresh egg noodles are best for this. If you are using fresh noodles, immerse them in a pot of boiling water and cook them for 3 to 5 minutes or until they are just soft. If you are using dried noodles, either cook them according to the instructions on the package, or cook them in boiling water for 4 to 5 minutes. Drain and serve.

If you are cooking noodles ahead of time before using them in another dish or before stir-frying them, toss the cooked, drained noodles in a teaspoon or two of sesame oil and put them into a bowl. Cover this with plastic wrap and put it in the refrigerator. The cooked noodles will remain usable for about 2 hours.

Udon

Udon are Japanese wheat noodles and can sometimes be found fresh at some supermarkets or Asian specialty markets. Round or flat, they can be purchased dried and should be cooked until they are soft but not overcooked, so they still retain a little bite.

Buckwheat noodles

These Japanese noodles are thin and a brownish grey color. Known as soba and extremely popular among the Japanese, they are often eaten as snacks, served cold in the summer and hot in the winter. They come fresh and dried, and can be found where Japanese food products are sold.

⊡ RICE NOODLES

Rice noodles are popular in southern China and throughout Southeast Asia. They are usually dried and can be found in Asian specialty markets. Rice noodles are white and come in a variety of shapes. One of the most common examples is rice stick noodles, which are flat and about the length of a chopstick. They can also vary in thickness. Use the type called for in the recipes. Rice noodles are very easy to use. Simply soak them in warm water for 15 minutes or until they are soft. Drain them in a colander or a sieve, and they are then ready to be used in soups or to be stir-fried. (The fresh ones, which also can be found in Asian specialty markets are a popular type called "fun noodles." These need to be cooked right away.)

Fun Rice Noodles

The Chinese make large sheets of rice noodles from a basic mixture of rice flour, wheat *starch* (not flour), and water. This pasta is then steamed in sheets. When cooked, the sheets are cut into noodles to be eaten immediately. A very popular street snack in China, Hong Kong, and Singapore, the fresh noodles are most often served with a sauce.

⊡ RICE PAPERS

Vietnamese rice papers are often beautifully textured by the imprint of the bamboo trays on which they are placed to dry. They are very thin dried sheets, usually round, and are used as wrappers for a Vietnamese-style spring roll. The dried sheets are very briefly soaked in water to soften them, then rolled around a filling and deep-fried to a light and crispy texture. Unlike the Chinese wrappers, the filled rice papers can be stored in the refrigerator for up to 3 hours before frying. Once they are fried, they can be kept crisp in a low oven for up to 2 hours.

☐ BEAN THREAD (TRANSPARENT) NOODLES

These noodles, also called cellophane noodles, are made from ground mung beans and not from a grain flour. They are available dried, and are very fine and white. Easy to recognize packed in their neat, plastic-wrapped bundles, they are stocked by most Asian specialty markets and some supermarkets. They are never served on their own, but are added to soups or braised dishes or are deep-fried as a garnish. They must be soaked in warm water for about 5 minutes before use. As they are rather long, you might find it easier to cut them into shorter lengths after soaking. They can also be fried, in which case, do not soak them before using.

CRISPY CANTONESE-STYLE NOODLES WITH VEGETABLES

½ pound dried or fresh thin
   Chinese egg noodles
1 ounce button mushrooms
6 whole scallions
¼ pound red pepper

 Serves 2 to 4

The origins of pasta are obscured by time and controversy, but there is a general consensus that the Chinese first thought of the egg noodle variety. Whoever invented the process, pan-fried noodles make a perfect foundation for stir-fried dishes. Here, the pan-frying technique

2 ounces celery
1⅓ cups chicken or vegetable
   stock
2 tablespoons peanut oil
4 garlic cloves, lightly
   crushed
¼ pound snow peas, trimmed
2 teaspoons light soy sauce
2 tablespoons oyster sauce
2 teaspoons sugar
3 tablespoons rice wine or
   dry sherry
2 teaspoons cornstarch mixed
   with 2 teaspoons water

leaves the noodles brown, firm and crispy on the outside, and yellow, moist and soft on the inside, a combination of texture that is classically Chinese. Upon this noodle base is placed a stir-fried vegetable topped by a zesty sauce. ■

Finely shred the mushrooms, scallions, and pepper. Coarsely chop the celery.

If you are using dried noodles, cook them according to the instructions on the package, otherwise boil for 2 minutes until soft. If you are using fresh Chinese noodles, boil for 3 minutes and then drain them thoroughly. Scatter the noodles in a baking pan.

Heat a large frying-pan, preferably non-stick and add 1 tablespoon of the oil. When hot, add the noodles and press down to make the noodles conform to the shape of the pan. Turn the heat to very low, and continue cooking for 10 to 15 minutes, until brown. Flip the noodles over in one piece and continue cooking them until the other side is brown. You may have to add a little oil or water from time to time to keep the noodles moist.

While the noodles are browning, heat a wok or large frying-pan until hot. Add the remaining oil and garlic and stir-fry for a few seconds. Put in the celery, mushrooms, and pepper and stir-fry for 3 minutes. Add the snow peas and scallions and continue to stir-fry for another 2 minutes. Stir in the soy sauce, oyster sauce, sugar, rice wine, and stock, and bring the mixture to a boil. Thicken this with the blended cornstarch until the sauce is cooked through.

Take out the noodles and place on a platter. Pour the vegetables and sauce over the noodles and serve at once.

FRESH PASTA WITH CORIANDER, GINGER, AND BASIL PESTO

PASTA

1¼ cups all-purpose flour
3 large eggs
2 tablespoons peanut oil
1 teaspoon salt

SAUCE

1 tablespoon finely chopped
   fresh ginger
1 tablespoon finely chopped
   fresh coriander
3 tablespoons finely chopped
   fresh basil
2 tablespoons finely chopped
   garlic
1 tablespoon peanut oil
2 teaspoons sesame oil
2 teaspoons salt
1 teaspoon freshly ground
   black pepper

Serves 6

This recipe was inspired by a colleague, Bruce Cost. A superb chef and author of excellent cook books, one of his specialties is the food of Southeast Asia. Here, I elaborate on a version of his delicious Asian pesto. Pesto is an Italian term meaning any sauce whose ingredients have been pounded and mixed together. The original Genoan pesto sauce consisted of fresh basil, parmesan cheese, oil, and garlic pounded into a smooth green paste. Ordinary fresh basil may be used here but, if you can, try to obtain the Asian tropical variety which has a distinctive basil-anise flavor worth tasting. Fresh coriander and ginger are, of course, traditional Asian seasonings. Combine this pesto with your own freshly made pasta, or buy dried or freshly made Chinese egg noodles. ■

For the pasta, by hand or in a food processor, combine the flour, eggs, oil, and salt. Knead the dough until it is smooth and satiny. Run the pasta through a pasta machine twice on each setting, stopping at the thinnest setting. Cut the pasta into thin noodles. Flour lightly and set aside.

Combine all the sauce ingredients and mix thoroughly in a blender and set aside.

Bring a large saucepan of water to a boil. Add the pasta and cook for 1 minute. Drain thoroughly and toss with the sauce. Serve at once.

SPICY BEAN THREAD NOODLES WITH DRIED SHRIMP

1 ounce Chinese dried
  mushrooms, finely chopped
6 ounces bean thread
  (transparent) noodles
2 ounces dried shrimp
2 tablespoons peanut oil
2 tablespoons finely chopped
  garlic
1 tablespoon finely chopped
  fresh ginger
2 tablespoons finely chopped
  shallots
2 teaspoons chili bean sauce
2 teaspoons light soy sauce
2 teaspons sugar
2 tablespoons rice wine or
  dry sherry
2 teaspoons chili oil

GARNISH

3 tablespoons finely chopped
  scallions, green part only

 Serves 2 to 4

These noodles have a smooth, light texture that readily absorbs the surrounding flavors. In this recipe, I follow my mother's example. Because most of the work involved can be done the day before, and because the dish reheats so well, this may be called gourmet fast food. After a hard day's work, my mother preferred to serve a meal that was easily prepared and yet tasty, and this is one of her favorites. The dried shrimp (page 30) may be found at most Asian specialty markets, but they can be omitted. I include them to preserve the authenticity of the recipe. Take care when cooking the noodles because if they overcook, they tend to lump together. Although the bean thread are known as noodles, this dish is also delicious served with rice. ■

Soak the dried mushrooms in warm water for 20 minutes. Drain them, squeeze out any excess liquid, cut off and discard the stalks and coarsely chop the mushroom caps. Soak the noodles in a large bowl of warm water for 15 minutes. When soft, drain the noodles well. Cut them into 3-inch lengths, using scissors or a knife. Soak the dried shrimp in a bowl of warm water for 15 minutes. When soft, drain the shrimp well.

Heat a wok or pan and add the oil. Put in the garlic, ginger, shallot, and chili bean sauce and stir-fry quickly for a few seconds. Add the shrimp, mushrooms, and noodles and stir-fry for about 2 minutes. Stir in the soy sauce, sugar, rice wine, and chili oil and continue to cook the mixture over a gentle heat for about 5 minutes. Ladle the noodles into a large serving bowl, garnish with the scallions and serve at once.

Singapore-style Rice Noodles

½ pound rice noodles, rice
    vermicelli, or rice sticks
¼ pound leeks
¼ pound carrots
¼ pound red peppers
1 ounce fresh chilies
4 scallions
2 tablespoons peanut oil
2 teaspoons salt
2 eggs, beaten
2 teaspoons sesame oil
½ teaspoon salt

SAUCE

2 tablespoons curry paste
1 tablespoon finely chopped
    garlic
1 tablespoon finely chopped
    fresh ginger
1⅓ cups chicken or vegetable
    stock
1 tablespoon sugar
2 tablespoons rice wine or
    dry sherry
2 tablespoons light soy sauce

GARNISH

fresh coriander leaves

 *Serves 2 to 4*

Rice noodles are lighter than wheat noodles and therefore lend themselves to dishes that are subtle and delicate. Singapore-style rice noodles are just such a treat. Whenever I visit Singapore or Hong Kong, I sample this popular favorite, and I am never disappointed. The recipe traditionally includes tiny fresh shrimp and shredded ham, and you may add some here if you wish, but this recipe is appetizing and pleasing vegetarian fare. The thin light noodles blend perfectly with the vegetables and the curry sauce. This is equally delicious warm or cold, which makes it perfect for a picnic. ■

Soak the rice noodles in a bowl of warm water for 25 minutes. Drain in a colander or sieve. (If you are using dried egg noodles, cook them for 3 to 5 minutes in boiling water, drain, and immerse them in cold water until required.)

Wash and finely shred the white part of the leeks. Finely shred the carrots, peppers, scallions and chili. In a small bowl, combine the eggs with the sesame oil and salt.

Heat a wok or large pan over a high heat and add the oil. When almost smoking, add the carrots, leeks, scallions, and salt and stir-fry for a few seconds. Add the peppers and stir-fry for about 1 minute. Put in the curry sauce ingredients and the drained noodles. Stir-fry the mixture for about 5 minutes until well mixed and heated through. Then add the egg mixture blending thoroughly. Stir-fry for 1 further minute. Serve at once, garnished with fresh coriander.

Spinach and Rice Noodles

1½ pounds fresh spinach
¼ pound rice noodles, rice
  vermicelli, or rice sticks
1 tablespoon peanut oil
2 teaspoons sugar
2 tablespoons coarsely
  chopped garlic
1 teaspoon salt
1 tablespoon light soy sauce
2 teaspoons chili oil

 Serves 2 to 4

In this quick and healthy light meal, the dried noodles need only to be soaked and require very little cooking. Their texture is such that the spinach flavor, some of the color and other seasonings are readily absorbed. Unlike egg noodles, rice noodles do not become sticky and gummy when they are moist; this makes it convenient to serve them cold. I add a little sugar to neutralize the iron and salt taste of the spinach. ■

Wash the spinach thoroughly. Remove all the stalks, leaving just the leaves.

Soak the rice noodles in a bowl of warm water for 25 minutes. Then drain them in a colander or sieve. (If you are using dried egg noodles, cook them for 3 to 5 minutes in boiling water, drain, and immerse in cold water until required.)

Heat a wok or large pan to moderate heat and add the oil. Put in the salt and garlic and stir-fry for a few seconds. Add the spinach leaves and stir-fry for 2 minutes to coat the spinach leaves thoroughly. When the spinach has wilted to about a third of its original size, add the rice noodles, sugar, soy sauce, and chili oil, and continue to stir-fry for another 4 minutes. Transfer the noodles to a plate, and pour off any excess liquid. Serve hot or cold.

TAN TAN NOODLES

1 tablespoon peanut oil
¼ pound Sichuan preserved
  vegetables, rinsed and
  finely chopped
1 tablespoon finely chopped
  garlic
2 teaspoons finely chopped
  fresh ginger
2 tablespoons rice wine or
  dry sherry
1 tablespoon chili bean sauce
1 tablespoon Chinese sesame
  paste or peanut butter
1 tablespoon dark soy sauce
1 tablespoon sugar
2 cups chicken or vegetable
  stock
½ pound Chinese fresh or
  dried flat thin wheat or egg
  noodles

Serves 2

To warm up on a cold afternoon or evening, serve Tan Tan noodles, which I first tasted in a Sichuan restaurant in Hong Kong. Given its Sichuan origin, I expected something spicy—but even so I was unprepared for its explosive quality. The noodles arrived preceded by a wonderful aroma and were served in a bowl shimmering with red chili oil. It was a delightful experience, featuring the classical spiciness of chili bean sauce, garlic, ginger, and Sichuan preserved vegetables. I immediately tried to recreate the noodles when I returned home. The result is this recipe, and I have enjoyed the noodles many times since. An essential ingredient is the Sichuan preserved vegetables; it is worth the search and can be found in cans at Asian specialty markets. The dish can still be made if you omit it, but the Sichuan preserved vegetables elevate the dish far above the ordinary. ■

Heat a wok or large frying-pan over high heat and add the oil. Put in the preserved vegetables, garlic, and ginger and stir-fry for 1 minute. Add the rice wine, chili bean sauce, sesame paste, soy sauce, sugar, and stock. Reduce the heat and simmer for 3 minutes over low heat.

Bring a large pot of water to boil and cook the noodles for 2 minutes if they are fresh and 5 minutes if dried. Drain well in a colander. Divide the noodles into individual bowls and ladle the sauce over them. Serve at once.

Hot and sour noodles

1 pound fresh or dried egg
   noodles
1 tablespoon sesame oil

SAUCE

2 tablespoons dark soy sauce
1 tablespoon chili oil
1 tablespoon Chinese black
   rice vinegar or cider
   vinegar
3 tablespoons finely chopped
   scallions
¼ teaspoon freshly ground
   black pepper
1 teaspoon sugar

 Serves 2 to 4

Hot and sour is a popular combination in Chinese cooking. We Chinese love the two compatible tastes on our palate. This type of noodles is often served in snack noodle shops or food stalls in China and Hong Kong. It serves as a quick fast-food meal that is full of flavor and easily made. I prefer to eat it hot, but it is also good cold. This makes a good, fast lunch dish. ▪

If you are using fresh noodles, cook first by boiling them for 3 to 5 minutes in a large pot of boiling water. If you are using dried noodles, cook in boiling water for 4 to 5 minutes. Drain the noodles, toss them in the sesame oil, and then put aside until required.

Heat all the sauce ingredients in a small saucepan. Turn the heat down to low and simmer for 5 minutes.

Plunge the noodles into boiling water for 20 seconds, then drain them well in a colander or sieve. Quickly tip the noodles into a large bowl and pour the hot sauce over the top. Mix everything together well and serve at once.

Udon noodles and broth

¾ pound dried udon noodles
½ pound fresh or canned
  tomatoes
8 scallions
1 quart chicken or vegetable
  stock
2 teaspoons salt
1 teaspoon freshly ground
  white pepper

Serves 4

During my student days, I became a devotee of Japanese films, especially those that incidentally depicted scenes from daily life. Such films gave me insight into a culture that I had only read about and never directly experienced. Naturally, I was particularly interested in scenes showing eating habits and cooking. I noticed that the Japanese often seemed to be snacking on soup noodles, slurping them up and smacking their lips in a way that always made me hungry. I later learned that they were probably udon noodles, a Japanese favorite. Made from bleached white flour with no eggs, these noodles are very white and fine and vary in thickness. In an easy soup such as this, they make a hearty lunch. ■

Cook the dried noodles in a saucepan of boiling water for 4 to 5 minutes or according to the instructions on the package. Drain the noodles, and then put them into cold water until required.

If you are using fresh tomatoes, peel, seed, and cut them into 1-inch cubes. If you are using canned tomatoes, chop them into small chunks.

Put the stock into a saucepan and bring it to a simmer. Add the salt and pepper and simmer for 2 minutes. Stir in the noodles and tomatoes and simmer until heated through. Add the scallions and simmer for 30 seconds more, then serve.

Singapore noodles

½ pound dried or fresh thin
   egg noodles
½ pound firm bean curd
1¼ cups peanut oil, for deep
   frying
2 teaspoons peanut oil
2 eggs, beaten
2 teaspoons sesame oil
½ teaspoon salt
2 tablespoons peanut oil
2 garlic cloves, crushed
2 tablespoons light soy sauce
2 teaspoons chili oil
3 tablespoons tomato paste
2 teaspoons sugar
2 tablespoons finely chopped
   scallions
1 fresh chili, seeded and
   shredded (optional)

 Serves 2

Singapore is a crossroads city in many ways, including the culinary. This delicious noodle recipe reflects just that with its combination of Indian, Thai, and Chinese influences. I enjoyed this dish during my first visit to Singapore when it became an instant favorite. The noodles used were slightly thicker than the thin fresh egg noodles used here. They contrast perfectly with the fried bean curd cubes, and the finished dish makes a tempting meal for two. ■

If you are using fresh noodles, blanch them first by boiling them for 3 to 5 minutes in a large saucepan of boiling water. If you are using the dried noodles, cook them in boiling water for 4 to 5 minutes. Drain the noodles, then put them into cold water until required. Cut the bean curd into ½-inch cubes.

Heat the 1⅓ cups oil in a deep-fat fryer or a large wok until it almost smokes. Deep-fry the bean curd cubes for 1 to 2 minutes in two batches. When each batch of bean curd cubes is lightly browned, remove and drain well on paper towel.

Heat the 2 teaspoons of oil in a wok or frying-pan and add the eggs, sesame oil, and salt. When cooked, the eggs should look like a thin, flat pancake. Remove from the pan, roll it up, and cut it in long 1-inch wide strips. Set aside.

Heat a wok or large frying-pan and add the 2 tablespoons of oil. When moderately hot, add the garlic and stir-fry for 30 seconds. Quickly drain the noodles and add them to the pan with the rest of the ingredients. Continue to stir-fry the noodles until all the ingredients are well mixed. Add the egg strips and bean curd and continue to stir-fry for another 3 to 4 minutes or until the bean curd is heated through.

KOREAN BEAN THREAD SESAME NOODLES WITH VEGETABLES

1 ounce Chinese dried
   mushrooms
½ ounce Chinese dried cloud
   ears (black fungus)
¼ pound bean thread
   (transparent) noodles
2 ounces carrot
1 green pepper
1 small onion
2 tablespoons peanut oil
½ cup water

SAUCE

2 tablespoons light soy
2 tablespoons dark soy sauce
3 tablespoons sesame oil
1½ tablespoons sesame seeds
1 tablespoon finely chopped
   garlic
1 tablespoon sugar
1 teaspoon freshly ground
   black pepper

 Serves 4

Bean thread noodles are made from the starch of the mung bean, and when cooked, they are almost translucent. This simple-to-prepare recipe is my version of a popular Korean dish. What makes it memorable is the combination of lace-like noodles and exotic mushrooms, an unusual mixture of tastes and textures. The dried mushrooms and cloud ears are available at Asian specialty markets and, because this is not an everyday dish, it is well worth the effort to obtain them. ▪

Soak the dried mushrooms in warm water for 20 minutes until soft. Squeeze the excess liquid from the mushrooms and remove and discard the stalks. Cut the caps into shreds. Soak the cloud ears in warm water for about 20 minutes or until soft. Rinse them well in cold water and drain them thoroughly in a colander.

Soak the noodles in a large bowl of very hot water for 15 minutes. When soft, drain well. Cut the noodles into 3-inch lengths, using scissors or a knife.

Peel and finely shred the carrot. Finely shred the pepper and onion.

Heat a wok or large frying-pan and add the oil. When moderately hot, add the mushrooms, cloud ears, carrot, onion, green pepper, and water and stir-fry for 5 minutes or until the carrots are cooked.

Combine the sauce ingredients and add them to the vegetables. Give the mixture a good stir, then add the noodles. Stir-fry the mixture for 2 minutes until well heated through. Serve at once or at room temperature.

Vegetarian chow mein

½ pound dried or fresh egg
 noodles

2 ounces celery

2 ounces canned bamboo
 shoots

2 tablespoons peanut oil

3 garlic cloves, crushed

1 small onion, finely sliced

½ pound small button
 mushrooms, whole

1 tablespoon light soy sauce

2 tablespoons dark soy sauce

2 teaspoons finely chopped
 fresh ginger

3 tablespoons chicken or
 vegetable stock

1 tablespoon rice wine or dry
 sherry

1 teaspoon sugar

¼ pound bean sprouts

GARNISH

fresh coriander sprigs

 Serves 4

Chow mein literally means "stir-fried noodles." It is a dish of universal popularity based upon the delicious combination of textures, tastes, and colors whether made with meat or, as in this case, with vegetables. Chow mein can be kept warm for at least an hour without losing any of its charm; I enjoy it cold. Serve as an economical family meal or at a buffet party. ▪

If you are using fresh noodles, blanch them first in a large pot of boiling water for 3 to 5 minutes. If you are using the dried noodles, cook in boiling water for 4 to 5 minutes. Drain the noodles, then put them into cold water until required.

String the celery and slice diagonally. Shred the bamboo shoots.

Heat a wok or large frying-pan and add the oil. When moderately hot, add the garlic and stir-fry for 10 seconds. Add the onion, mushrooms, celery, and bamboo shoots and stir-fry for about 5 minutes. Drain the noodles thoroughly and put into the wok. Continue to stir-fry for 1 minute then add the rest of the ingredients except the bean sprouts. Continue to stir-fry for another 2 minutes and then add the bean sprouts. Give the mixture a good stir and turn it onto a serving platter.

Garnish with the fresh coriander sprigs.

Stir-Fried Vegetables Over a Rice Noodle Cloud

1¼ cups peanut oil, for deep-frying oil

6 ounces rice noodles, rice vermicelli or rice sticks

4 scallions

¾ pound eggplant

½ pound zucchini

3 garlic cloves, crushed

2 tablespoons rice wine or dry sherry

2 tablespoons yellow bean sauce

2 teaspoons chili bean sauce

⅔ cup chicken or vegetable stock

1 teaspoon cornstarch mixed with 1 teaspoon water

1 teaspoon sugar

2 tablespoons dark soy sauce

1 teaspoon salt

 Serves 4 to 6

At Chinese banquets when I was a child, the food we children enjoyed most were the dishes that featured fried rice noodles. I believe this is still true today for Western children whose parents take them to Chinese restaurants. Practically any stir-fried dish with a little sauce makes a wonderful topping for these crisp, crackling, crunchy noodles. In this recipe, I combine them with slightly spiced vegetables, enhanced with aromatic seasonings. ■

Heat the oil in a deep-fat fryer or large wok, until very hot. Deep-fry the noodles until they are crisp and puffed up. Remove with a slotted spoon and drain on paper towel. You may have to do this in several batches.

Cut the eggplant and zucchini into 3-inch lengths. Sprinkle them with salt and leave them in a sieve to drain for 20 minutes. Rinse under cold running water and pat dry with paper towel.

Heat a wok or large frying-pan and add 1½ tablespoons of the oil in which you have fried the noodles. When moderately hot, add the garlic and scallions and stir-fry for 30 seconds. Add the eggplant and zucchini and continue to stir-fry for 1 minute. Stir in the rest of the ingredients except the cornstarch mixture and continue to cook for 3 minutes. Finally, add the blended cornstarch and continue to cook for 1 minute.

Place the deep-fried noodles on a platter and spoon the vegetables over the top. Serve immediately.

LIGHT AND EASY RICE NOODLES

½ pound dried flat rice
noodles or ½ recipe of
fresh rice "fun" noodles
(page 149)

SAUCE

2 tablespoons hoisin sauce
1½ tablespoons light soy
sauce
2 teaspoons chili bean sauce
1 tablespoon sesame oil

GARNISH

1 tablespoon toasted sesame
seeds (page 30)

 Serves 2

Making my way through the streets of Hong Kong and other Asian cities, I have often paused at curbside food stalls to enjoy this "fast food" dish. It is light but sustaining and easy to digest as you go about your business. This recipe makes a quick lunch for two using either fresh or dried flat rice noodles. ■

If you are using the dried rice noodles, bring a large saucepan of water to a boil, remove it from the heat and add the rice noodles. Let them stand for about 10 minutes, then drain thoroughly. If you are using the fresh rice noodles, set up a steamer or fill a wok or deep casserole with at least 2 inches of water. Put a rack into the wok or casserole and bring the water to a boil. Put the rice noodles onto a deep plate and lower the plate into the steamer or onto the rack. Cover the wok tightly. Gently steam on a low heat for 15 to 20 minutes.

Combine the sauce ingredients and pour over the softened or steamed noodles. Garnish with the sesame seeds and serve.

Homemade Chinese Rice "Fun" Noodles with Peppers

6 ounces yellow peppers
6 ounces red peppers
4 ounces green peppers
2 tablespoons peanut oil
3 garlic cloves, crushed
1 pound fresh "fun" noodles
  (page 165)
1 tablespoon yellow bean
  sauce
2 tablespoons oyster sauce
1 tablespoon rice wine or dry
  sherry
2 tablespoons finely chopped
  scallions
⅔ cup chicken or vegetable
  stock
1 teaspoon sugar

 Serves 4

Occasionally, on hot, humid Chicago summer evenings when my mother was understandably not in the mood for cooking, she would send me out to a local Chinese restaurant for some "chow fun." "Fun" are freshly made, soft, tender rice noodles which are usually combined with beef and bitter melon or beef and peppers. Either way, it was delicious. This is my vegetarian version of the dish, and it is as much fun to prepare and to eat as the original. The texture of the noodles is a good contrast to that of the colorful, zesty peppers. Once the noodles are made, the rest is a simple stir-fry. Try adding chopped black beans as an experiment. ■

Cut the peppers into ½-inch squares.

Heat a wok or large frying-pan and add the oil. When moderately hot, add the garlic and stir-fry for about 30 seconds. Add the noodles, peppers, yellow bean sauce, oyster sauce, rice wine, scallions, stock, and sugar, and stir-fry for about 3 minutes or until the peppers are thoroughly cooked. Turn out on a large serving platter and serve at once.

Homemade Chinese Fresh Rice "Fun" Noodles

1 cup rice flour
6 tablespoons wheat starch
½ teaspoon salt
1¼ cups water
About 2 tablespoons
  peanut oil
1 tablespoon sesame oil

 Makes about 1 pound fresh rice "fun" noodles

As a young apprentice working in my uncle's restaurant kitchen, I was always fascinated by his skill in making fresh rice noodles. He would make up the batter in the evening and then come in very early the next morning before the restaurant opened to steam the batter into noodles, using five enormous woks. I have never forgotten how he managed to keep all the woks going at once, skipping quickly from one to the other. Freshly made rice noodles are very tasty, with a smooth, soft texture and a velvety surface that combines well with a light coating of sauce, as pasta should.

You should try making your own noodles a few times, if only to see if the freshly made ones are superior to the packaged version. The rice flour and the wheat starch (not the same thing as wheat flour) are readily available at Asian specialty markets. The steaming technique assures a moist rice sheet that is easily rolled to be cut into noodles. Be sure to oil the steaming tin each time you add new batter, to prevent sticking. Once rolled and tightly wrapped, the sheets will keep in the refrigerator for at least two days so you can cut the noodles just before you need to use them. Having mastered the technique and tasted the fresh noodles, I am sure you will make them often. Some Asian specialty markets carry ready-made fresh "fun" noodles. ▪

In a large bowl, combine the rice flour, wheat starch, salt, and water. Stir the batter until it is smooth and strain it through a fine sieve. Stir in the oil and sesame oil. Let the batter rest for 30 minutes.

Set up a steamer by adding 2 inches water to a wok or deep pan and bring it to a simmer. Lightly oil a round baking tin which fits easily into the wok or pan.

Give the batter a good stir and add 5 or 6 tablespoons of the mixture to the baking tin. Gently tip it so that the batter coats the surface of the tin. Place the tin into the wok or pan so that it sits uncovered above the simmering water and cover the wok tightly. Steam gently for 3 to 4 minutes or until the batter is cooked. Remove the baking tin and allow it to cool slightly. Gently roll up the rice sheet and repeat the process until all the batter is used up.

Cover the rolled up rice sheets with plastic wrap and refrigerate at least 1 hour before cutting. Cut the sheets into ½-inch wide noodles and use immediately. The "fun" noodles can be steamed and then topped with a sauce or stir-fried.

Cold Pasta & Noodles

Asian pasta is delicious hot or cold. When you prepare the noodles in this chapter, make them in basically the same way you would prepare the hot noodles. The noodle recipes here are a sampling of my favorite cold noodle treats. They are ideal for simple buffets and for picnics and are more than merely adequate alternatives to hot pasta or noodle dishes.

I include here Spicy Black Bean Sauce Noodles and Cold Sichuan Noodles, which reflect the hot and spicy Chinese style, and Southeast Asian Noodle Salad and Cold Curry-Flavored Noodles, which deliciously show the creativity of other regional styles. Because cold temperatures affect the potency of spices, it is best to experiment with these recipes to discover your own personal preference.

COLD CHINESE NOODLE SALAD WITH MUSHROOMS

½ pound fresh or dried thin
  Chinese egg noodles
1 tablespoon peanut oil
2 garlic cloves, crushed
2 tablespoons rice wine or
  dry sherry
1 tablespoon light soy sauce
½ pound small button
  mushrooms

DRESSING

½ teaspoon freshly ground
  black pepper
3 tablespoons finely chopped
  scallions
1 tablespoon finely chopped
  fresh ginger
1½ tablespoons light soy
  sauce
2 tablespoons peanut oil
1 tablespoon sesame oil

 Serves 2

This is a simple dish that unites two satisfying foods, noodles and mushrooms, in a most appetizing sauce. Hot oils are poured over ginger and scallions, releasing their tangy flavors; the sauce is allowed to cool, then mixed with the noodles. The mushrooms are cooked separately to preserve their texture. ▪

If you are using fresh noodles, blanch first in a large saucepan of boiling water for 3 to 5 minutes. Immerse them in cold water. If you are using the dried noodles, cook them in boiling water for 4 to 5 minutes. Drain the noodles, then put them into cold water until required.

Heat a wok or large frying-pan and add the oil. When moderately hot, add the garlic and stir-fry for 30 seconds. Stir in the rice wine, soy sauce, and whole button mushrooms and stir-fry for 3 minutes or until the mushrooms are cooked. Remove from the wok and set aside. Wipe the wok clean.

Combine all the dressing ingredients, except the oils, in a small heatproof bowl. Reheat the wok and add both oils until they begin to smoke. Pour this mixture over the dressing ingredients which are in the bowl. Drain the noodles thoroughly in a colander. In a large bowl, combine the noodles, mushrooms, and dressing. Mix well and serve immediately or within 3 hours.

CUCUMBER NOODLE SALAD

¼ pound bean thread
   (transparent) noodles
½ pound cucumbers

DRESSING

3 tablespoons light soy sauce
2 tablespoons Chinese white
   rice vinegar or cider
   vinegar
2 teaspoons chili oil
1 tablespoon sugar
1 tablespoon peanut oil
2 teaspoons finely chopped
   fresh ginger
3 tablespoons finely chopped
   scallions

 Serves 2

This is a simple vegetarian dish, ideal for warm weather meals. The bean thread noodles have a satiny smooth texture and their light flavor goes well with cucumbers, dressed in a piquant hot and sour sauce. ◼

Soak the noodles in a large bowl of very hot water for 5 minutes. Drain and immerse them in cold water, then drain thoroughly in a colander. Cut the noodles into 3-inch lengths using scissors or a knife.

   Peel the cucumbers, slice them in half lengthways and, using a teaspoon, remove the seeds. Cut the cucumber halves into 3-inch lengths, ¼ inch thick.

   In a large bowl, combine the dressing ingredients, then add the cucumbers and noodles. Mix thoroughly. Turn the salad onto a serving platter, and serve immediately or within 3 hours.

Spicy black bean sauce noodles

¾ pound fresh or dried
   Chinese egg noodles

SAUCE

3 tablespoons peanut oil

2 tablespoons yellow bean
   sauce

2 tablespoons black beans,
   coarsely chopped

2 tablespoons finely chopped
   garlic

1 tablespoon finely chopped
   fresh ginger

2 tablespoons finely chopped
   scallions

2 teaspoons chili bean sauce

2 teaspoons sugar

1 tablespoon dark soy sauce

2 teaspoons chili oil

2 tablespoons rice wine or
   dry sherry

5 ounces chicken or vegetable
   stock

1 teaspoon cornstarch mixed
   with 1 teaspoon water

 Serves 2

Ever since I can remember, the aroma of black beans cooked with garlic has meant mouth-watering food. Because I enjoy cold noodles, I have adapted these seasonings for a light lunch dish or warm summer evening dinner. The pungent sauce is cooked beforehand and allowed to cool before enlivening the cold noodles. ■

If you are using fresh noodles, blanch in a large saucepan of boiling water for 3 to 5 minutes, then immerse them in cold water. If you are using the dried noodles, cook in boiling water for 4 to 5 minutes. Drain the noodles, then put into cold water until required.

For the sauce, heat a wok or large frying-pan and add the oil. When moderately hot, add the yellow bean sauce, black beans, garlic, ginger, and scallions and stir-fry for 2 minutes. Then add the rest of the ingredients except the cornstarch mixture, and continue to cook for 2 minutes. Stir in the blended cornstarch and bring to a boil for 30 seconds. Remove from the heat and allow the sauce to cool. Drain the noodles thoroughly in a colander and mix with the sauce. Serve at once.

COLD CURRY-FLAVORED NOODLES

1 pound dried or fresh
   Chinese egg noodles

DRESSING

1 tablespoon peanut oil
2 tablespoons finely chopped
   garlic
1 tablespoon finely chopped
   onion
1¼ cups fresh or canned
   coconut milk (page 20)
½ teaspoon turmeric
2 tablespoons curry paste
1 teaspoon salt
1 teaspoon sugar
2 tablespoons light soy sauce

GARNISH

fresh basil or fresh coriander
   leaves

 Serves 2 to 4

Cold noodles can take strong flavors, because the coldness mutes tastes. Here, I have used Southeast Asian spices and seasonings and created a curry sauce strong enough to enliven the cold noodles. The sauce is cooked to bring out its full range of tastes, then cooled before mixing with the noodles. I like to serve these curried noodles with grilled meats; they also make a noteworthy side dish for many family meals. ■

If you are using dried noodles, cook them according to the instructions on the package or else boil them for 4 to 5 minutes. Immerse in cold water until required. If you are using fresh Chinese noodles, boil them for 3 to 5 minutes, then cool them in cold water.

Heat a wok or pan and add the oil. When moderately hot, add the garlic and onion and stir-fry for 2 minutes. Stir in the coconut milk, turmeric, curry paste, salt, sugar, and soy sauce and simmer for 4 minutes. Allow the dressing mixture to cool.

Drain the noodles thoroughly and toss with the dressing. Turn onto a platter, garnish with the fresh herbs, and serve within 3 hours.

Sesame buckwheat noodles

1 pound dried thin Japanese
buckwheat soba noodles
(page 149)

DRESSING

1 tablespoon chili oil
2 tablespoons sesame oil
1 tablespoon peanut oil
3 tablespoons dashi (page 22)
or chicken or vegetable
stock
2 teaspoons sugar
2 tablespoons light soy sauce
½ teaspoon salt

GARNISH

2 tablespoons toasted sesame
seeds (page 30)
2 tablespoons scallion tops,
thinly diagonally sliced

 Serves 2

This simple dish is adapted from a traditional Japanese recipe. The
buckwheat noodles have a unique texture that remains excellent when
served cold. Perhaps this is because buckwheat, with a different struc-
ture from wheat or millet, is not a true cereal. I prefer to use the thin
buckwheat noodles for their lightness. This recipe will make a satisfying lunch for two. ■

Cook the dried noodles according to the instructions on the package
or boil them for 4 to 5 minutes. Drain, then cool in cold water until
required.

Combine the dressing ingredients together in a bowl. Drain the
noodles thoroughly and toss them with the dressing. Garnish with the
sesame seeds and scallion tops and serve.

Southeast asian noodle salad

½ pound flat rice noodles
2 scallions
2 ounces snow peas
2 ounces carrots
¼ pound bean sprouts

DRESSING

2 tablespoons fresh lime juice
2 teaspoons chili oil
1½ tablespoons light soy
    sauce
2 teaspoons sesame oil
1 tablespoon lemon juice
6 tablespoons fresh or canned
    coconut milk (page 20)
½ teaspoon salt
grated rind of 1 lime
1 teaspoon fish sauce
½ teaspoon freshly ground
    black pepper
1 tablespoon sugar
2 tablespoons finely chopped
    fresh coriander
1½ tablespoons finely
    chopped fresh ginger
4 tablespoons finely chopped
    fresh basil

GARNISH

3 tablespoons roasted
    peanuts, coarsely chopped

 Serves 4

On my first visit to Southeast Asia many years ago, what most impressed me was the use of exotic and fascinating combinations of ingredients such as coconut milk, limes, fish sauce, and herbs such as basil, all of which were foreign to my tradition. I have since become familiar with these and other once strange ingredients, and my experiments have led me to some very delectable results, as with this light lunch or supper noodle dish, which includes an aromatic combination of splendid tastes and colors. ■

Bring a large saucepan of water to a boil, remove from the heat, and add the rice noodles. Let them sit for about 15 minutes, then drain, and immerse them in cold water until required.

Finely shred the scallions, snow peas, and carrots. Bring a pan of water to the boil and blanch the bean sprouts, scallions, snow peas, and carrots for 1 minute. Immerse immediately in cold water, drain, and set aside.

Combine all the ingredients for the dressing mixture. Drain the noodles thoroughly and toss them with the dressing mixture and the vegetables. Garnish with the peanuts and serve within 3 hours.

Cold sichuan noodles

1 pound dried or fresh
  Chinese egg noodles
2 tablespoons peanut oil
2 tablespoons finely chopped
  scallions
1 tablespoon finely chopped
  garlic
1 tablespoon yellow bean
  sauce
2 teaspoons chili bean sauce
2 teaspoons finely chopped
  fresh ginger
1 tablespoon rice wine or dry
  sherry
2 tablespoons dark soy sauce
2 tablespoons sesame oil

GARNISH

fresh coriander leaves

 Serves 2

In this Chinese recipe for spicy noodles, traditionally served hot, I have simply directed that it be eaten cold. This makes a delectable cold salad for warm weather days. It is an ideal luncheon dish for two, but the portions may be increased easily for use in a family meal. ∎

If using the dried noodles, cook them according to package instructions or else boil them for 4 to 5 minutes. Cool in cold water until required. If using the fresh noodles, boil them for 3 to 5 minutes, then immerse in cold water.

Heat a wok or large frying-pan and add the oil. When hot, add the scallions, garlic, yellow bean sauce, chili bean sauce, and ginger and stir-fry for 2 minutes. Allow the mixture to cool thoroughly.

Drain the noodles and combine them with the cool seasonings, soy sauce, and sesame oil. Garnish with the coriander and serve within 3 hours.

Fragrant noodle salad

½ pound flat rice noodles
½ pound tomatoes
2 ounces red onions

DRESSING

rind of 1 lime, finely chopped
2 tablespoons lime juice
2 tablespoons light soy sauce
1 tablespoon sugar
1 tablespoon peanut oil
2 teaspoons finely chopped
   garlic
1 teaspoon chili oil
1 teaspoon finely chopped
   fresh lemongrass
2 tablespoons finely chopped
   fresh coriander
2 tablespoons finely chopped
   fresh basil
1 tablespoon finely chopped
   fresh mint

 Serves 2

This is a refreshing noodle salad from Southeast Asia. Although tomatoes are not indigenous to the region, they have completely won over Asian cooks since their introduction a century ago, and for good reason: they are flavorful, colorful, and nutritious. Except for the Eastern dressing ingredients, this could pass for a zesty Italian pasta dish. ■

Bring a large saucepan of water to the boil, remove from the heat, and add the rice noodles. Let them sit for about 15 minutes, then drain and immerse in cold water until required.

If you are using fresh tomatoes, peel, seed, and coarsely chop them. If you are using canned tomatoes, coarsely chop. Finely slice the onions.

Combine all the dressing ingredients except for the fresh herbs. Thoroughly drain the noodles and toss them with the dressing, herbs, tomatoes, and onions. Serve within 3 hours.

Spicy Citrus-Flavored Noodles

½ pound fresh or dried
   Chinese egg noodles
1 tablespoon sesame oil

SAUCE

1 dried red chili
2 teaspoons peanut oil
2 teaspoons sesame paste or
   peanut butter
2 tablespoons orange juice
2 teaspoons lemon juice
grated rind of 1 orange
granted rind of 1 lemon
1 teaspoon finely chopped
   scallions
1 teaspoon finely chopped
   garlic
1 tablespoon Chinese white
   rice vinegar or cider
   vinegar
1 tablespoon dark soy sauce
2 teaspoons sugar
¼ teaspoon Sichuan
   peppercorns
2 teaspoons chili oil

 *Serves 2 to 4*

This versatile dish is perfect for warm weather eating, picnics, or large-scale entertaining. The egg noodles are a natural foil for the zest of the orange and lemon and combine perfectly with the spicy peanut sauce. Mix the noodles with the sauce *only* when you are about to serve the dish. If you prefer the sauce to be even spicier, simply add more chili oil and garlic. ■

If using dried noodles, cook them according to the package instructions or boil for 4 to 5 minutes. Cool in cold water until required. If using fresh noodles, cook the noodles by boiling for 3 to 5 minutes then immerse in cold water. In the same hot water, blanch the dried chili until soft. Then blanch the lemon and orange rind for 30 seconds to remove their bitterness.

    Mix the sauce ingredients together with the chili in a bowl or in an electric blender. (This can be done in advance and kept refrigerated, as the sauce is served cold.)

    Drain the cooked noodles, toss them with the sesame oil, and arrange on a platter or in a large bowl. Toss the noodles well with the sauce just before serving.

Rice

Rice is the staple food of most of China, Southeast Asia and Japan. Unlike bread, a Western staple that plays only a secondary role in Western cooking, rice is an integral part of every Asian meal and is eaten many times during the day. Left-over rice is stir-fried or dried to use in rice cakes, simmered in a rice porridge, or simply eaten as a snack. Like bean curd, rice combines well with other foods and flavors. Somewhat bland by itself, it readily absorbs other tastes.

Each country treats rice in a different way, ranging from Thai Aromatic Fried Rice to the simple, austere Japanese Rice with Asparagus. Although there are numerous varieties of rice in the world, for everyday use we need only be concerned with three: long-grain, short-grain, and glutinous.

⊡ LONG-GRAIN RICE

This is the most popular rice for Asian food and is my own favorite. Although the Chinese still go through the ritual of washing it, I believe this step can be bypassed with rice purchased at supermarkets. Do not confuse it with "easy-cook" and precooked varieties which are widely available. They are unsuitable for the recipes in this book, except for those using coconut milk which is rich in fats. Try to obtain the Thai aromatic long-grain rice, now available at many Asian specialty markets. It has a pleasing fragrance similar to the basmati rice used in Indian cuisine.

To wash rice

This is an optional step. Put the required amount of rice into a large bowl, fill it with cold water, and swish the rice around with your hands. Carefully pour off the cloudy water, keeping the rice in the bowl. Repeat this process several times until the water is clear.

To cook long-grain rice

These basic instructions for long-grain rice are easy and foolproof and always produce excellent results.

2 cups long-grain rice

Put the rice into a large bowl and, if you wish, wash it in several changes of water until the water becomes clear. (This step may be omitted.) Drain the rice and put it into a heavy pan with 3½ cups water and bring to a boil. Continue boiling until most of the surface liquid has evaporated. This should take about 15 to 20 minutes. The surface of the rice should have small indentations like a pitted crater. At this point, cover the pan with a very tightfitting lid, turn the heat as low as possible and let the rice cook undisturbed for 15 to 20 minutes. There is no need to "fluff" the rice before serving it, but it should be thoroughly cooled before stir-frying.

A few rules are worth repeating in regard to long-grain rice:

- The water should be at a level 1 inch above the surface of the rice; too much water means gummy rice. Recipes on commercial packages generally recommend too much water.
- Never uncover the pan once the simmering process has begun; time the process and wait.

▫ SHORT-GRAIN RICE

This rice is not to be confused with pudding rice. Short-grain rice, usually used in Chinese cooking for making porridge, is more popular in Japan. Varieties known as "American Rose" or "Japanese Rose" are very suitable and can be found in many Asian specialty markets or in shops that carry Japanese food products. Short-grain is slightly stickier than long-grain white rice, but is cooked the same way.

▫ GLUTINOUS RICE

Glutinous rice is also known as sweet or sticky rice. It is short, round, and pearl-like, and is not to be confused with ordinary short-grain or pudding rice. It has more gluten than ordinary rice, and when cooked is stickier and sweeter. It is used for substantial rice dishes such as Steamed Sticky Rice or in stuffings, desserts, and for making Chinese rice wine and vinegar. Most Asian specialty markets stock it. Glutinous rice must be soaked at least 2 hours (preferably overnight) before cooking. You may cook it in the same way as long-grain rice.

CORN AND GINGER FRIED RICE

1 pound fresh corn on the
    cob, or 1¼ cups canned
    corn, plain
1 tablespoon peanut oil
1½ tablespoons finely
    chopped fresh ginger
2 tablespoons finely chopped
    scallions
2 tablespoons rice wine or
    dry sherry
2 cups long-grain rice, cooked
¼ teaspoon salt
¼ teaspoon freshly ground
    pepper
2 tablespoons sesame oil

Corn and rice go well together, with their contrasting and comple-mentary textures, colors, and flavors. The addition of ginger makes them a bit exotic—a true East-West delight. Use fresh corn if possible, and be sure the cooked rice is cold before stir-frying. This will keep it from absorbing too much oil and becoming sticky. This economical and healthful dish may be eaten as a rice salad or as a vegetable ac-companiment to other foods. ■

Remove the corn kernels with a sharp knife or cleaver. You should end up with about 1¼ cups. If you are using canned corn, empty the contents into a sieve, drain well, and set aside.

Heat a wok or large frying-pan until hot and add the oil. Put in the ginger and scallions and stir-fry for a few seconds. Add the rice wine and continue to stir-fry a few more seconds. Stir in the cold cooked rice and stir-fry for 5 minutes, then add the corn, salt, and pepper, and continue to stir-fry for 2 minutes. Finally, add the sesame oil and stir-fry for 4 more minutes until the corn is thoroughly cooked. Serve at once, or cold as a rice salad.

Steamed sticky rice

2 cups glutinous or short-grained rice
½ cup dried shrimp (optional)
¼ pound fresh or frozen peas
¼ pound button mushrooms
1 tablespoon peanut oil
1 tablespoon finely chopped fresh ginger
3 tablespoons finely chopped scallions
2 tablespoons finely chopped Sichuan preserved vegetables
3 tablespoons rice wine or dry sherry
1 tablespoon oyster sauce
2 tablespoons light soy sauce

 Serves 4

In this recipe, the rice is scented with the many seasonings which are slowly steamed along with it. This is a dish my mother used to cook for me on those days when she could not be home to prepare lunch. She would make the dish and then set it in the warm steamer where all the ingredients would slowly marry. ■

Put the rice in a large bowl, cover with water, and let it sit for 4 hours or overnight. Drain well. Set up a steamer or put a rack inside a wok or large, deep pan. Pour in about 2 inches water and bring it to a boil. Put the rice in a bowl and place this into the steamer or onto the rack. Cover the pan tightly, turn the heat low, and steam gently for about 20 minutes.

If you are using dried shrimp, soak them in warm water for 20 minutes. Drain and discard the water. If you are using fresh peas, blanch in a pan of boiling water for 3 minutes; drain well. Immerse in cold water to stop them from cooking. Finely slice the mushrooms.

Heat a wok or large frying-pan and add the oil. When moderately hot, put in the ginger, scallions and shrimp and stir-fry for 2 minutes. Add the mushrooms and Sichuan preserved vegetables and continue to cook for 5 minutes or until most of the liquid has evaporated. Add the rice wine, oyster sauce, and soy sauce and continue to cook for 2 minutes. Stir in the steamed rice and peas.

Replenish the steamer with hot water. Transfer the rice mixture into a bowl and steam for another 30 minutes over low heat. It is now ready to be served. This rice can be kept warm in the steamer, with the heat turned off, for 25 minutes. It also reheats well.

THAI AROMATIC FRIED RICE

2 tablespoons peanut oil
¼ pound onion, finely
    chopped
2 cups long-grain rice, cooked
¼ teaspoon salt
1 tablespoon fish sauce
2 teaspoons chili bean sauce
3 tablespoons tomato paste
3 tablespoons finely chopped
    scallions
2 tablespoons finely chopped
    fresh coriander
4 eggs, beaten

Serves 4

Thai cuisine has been influenced by the Chinese, but there is a great deal of originality in the Thai tradition. This recipe is distinctly Thai, as the combination of fish sauce and chili bean sauce is not normally used with rice in Chinese cooking. The pungent flavor of the fish sauce mellows when it is cooked, leaving a fragrant aroma. The result is an unusually zesty rice dish. You may stir-fry the cooked rice without waiting for it to cool. ■

Heat a wok or large frying-pan and add the oil. When moderately hot, add the onion and stir-fry for 3 minutes. Put in the rice and continue to stir-fry for another 3 minutes. Add the rest of the ingredients, except the eggs. Stir-fry the mixture for 5 minutes over a high heat. Next add the beaten eggs and cook for 3 minutes or until the eggs have set. Turn the mixture onto a platter and serve.

Hᴏɴɢ ᴋᴏɴɢ–sᴛʏʟᴇ ꜰʀɪᴇᴅ ʀɪᴄᴇ

2 tablespoons peanut oil
½ pound fresh broccoli or
   Chinese broccoli
¼ pound fresh or frozen peas
1 teaspoon salt
2 tablespoons water
2 cups long-grain rice, cooked
2 eggs, beaten
2 teaspoons sesame oil

 Serves 4

One of the many memorable meals I have enjoyed in Hong Kong included a dish of rice, stir-fried with Chinese broccoli stalks and eggs. I first sampled it in the delightful company of the eminent food critic, Willie Mark, who guided me to the restaurant that served it. Ordinary Western broccoli also works well in this recipe. ■

Separate the broccoli heads into florets. Peel the stalks if necessary. Dice the broccoli into very small pieces.

If you are using fresh peas, blanch them in a small saucepan of boiling water for 2 minutes; if you are using frozen peas, blanch 1 minute.

Heat a wok or large frying-pan and add the oil. When moderately hot, add the broccoli, peas, and salt and stir-fry for about 1 minute, then add the water. Continue to stir-fry the mixture for about 2 minutes or until the broccoli is cooked. Add the cold cooked rice and stir-fry for 3 minutes. Then add the eggs and sesame oil and stir-fry for another 2 minutes. Turn the mixture onto a platter and serve at once.

CHINESE RICE PORRIDGE WITH CONDIMENTS

1 quart chicken or vegetable
  stock
2 cups short-grain rice
2 teaspoons salt

GARNISH

1 garlic clove
2 scallions
1 fresh chili
1 tablespoon finely chopped
  fresh coriander
1 tablespoon light soy sauce
1 egg
1 teaspoon chili oil
¼ pound fresh or canned
  tomatoes
2 tablespoons roasted peanuts
  (page 26)

 Serves 2

Porridge in the West is a plain yet sustaining dish; in Eastern cookery, porridge is soothing, warm, and aromatic. Chinese porridge is usually quite tasty, depending on the flavorings added, and Malaysian porridge is always fiery. This lunch dish is based upon Malaysian porridge the seasonings being especially typical of this cuisine. I like to place the garnish around the porridge before stirring it in because it looks so attractive. ■

Bring the stock to the boil in a large saucepan and add the rice and salt. Return the mixture to a boil and give it several good stirs. Turn the heat down to low and cover the pan. Simmer for about 45 minutes, stirring occasionally to keep it from sticking.

Arrange the garnishes on a separate platter. When you are ready to serve the porridge, add the garnishes and serve at once.

Fragrant coconut rice

2 tablespoons peanut oil
½ pound finely chopped
  onion
2 cups long-grain rice or
  "easy cook" rice, cooked
1 teaspoon turmeric
2 teaspoons salt
2 cups fresh or canned
  coconut milk (page 20)
⅔ cup chicken or vegetable
  stock
2 whole cloves
1 whole cinnamon stick or
  Chinese cinnamon bark
2 bay leaves

Serves 4

For this recipe you may use "easy-cook" rice. It is one of those rare dishes in which such pre-cooked rice works well, partly because of the richness and oils in the coconut.

Unusual as the combination of spices may seem, you will find them a harmonious blend with this dish. If you use long-grain rice, it will be a bit sticky, as it should be. The rice reheats well but should be warmed over a very low heat. ▪

Heat the oil in a large casserole until moderately hot. Add the onion and stir-fry for 2 minutes. Put in the rice, turmeric, and salt, and continue to cook for 2 minutes.

Add the coconut milk and stock and bring the mixture to a boil. Stir in the whole cloves, cinnamon, and bay leaves. Turn the heat as low as possible and let the rice cook undisturbed for 20 minutes. It is ready to serve when the rice is cooked.

TWO MUSHROOM RICE

1 ounce Chinese dried
   mushrooms
3½ cups very hot water
½ pound fresh button
   mushrooms
1 tablespoon peanut oil
3 tablespoons finely chopped
   scallions
½ teaspoon salt
2 tablespoons light soy sauce
2 cups long-grained rice

Serves 4

This is a simple vegetarian adaptation of a traditional chicken-rice-mushroom dish my mother often made when I was a child. Even without the chicken, it remains a favorite of mine. One must properly appreciate the mushroom which, in the words of a discriminating scholar, "belongs to that category of plants used in cooking whose main function is to add less flavor than the spices and herbs, less bulk than the real vegetables, and to absorb differentially the flavors of the dish, in order to bring out, by subtle chemistry, the highest and most delicate tastes." Once you begin to think of mushrooms in this way and to use them accordingly, all mushroom dishes take on a special charm and flavor. Save the water in which the dried mushrooms have been soaked, as it gives an additional earthy flavor to the cooked rice. ■

Soak the dried mushrooms in 3½ cups very hot water for 20 minutes until soft. Remove them with a slotted spoon and save the liquid. Squeeze the excess liquid from the mushrooms and remove and discard the stalks. Cut the caps into quarters. Cut the button mushrooms into quarters.

Heat a wok or large frying-pan and add the oil. When hot, add the scallions, salt, and button mushrooms and stir-fry for 2 minutes. Put in the dried mushrooms and stir-fry for another minute or until all the liquid has evaporated. Remove the mixture and set aside.

Add the mushrooms, soy sauce, and mushroom liquid to the rice in a pan and bring it to a boil. Continue boiling until most of the surface liquid has evaporated. This should take about 15 to 20 minutes. At this point, cover the pan with a very tight-fitting lid, turn the heat as low as possible, and let the rice cook undisturbed with the mushrooms for 15 to 20 minutes.

CURRIED FRIED RICE WITH GREEN BEANS

2 tablespoons peanut oil
¼ pound Chinese long-beans, runner beans, or haricots verts, trimmed and diced
2 cups long-grain rice, cooked
1 tablespoon finely chopped garlic
3 tablespoons finely chopped fresh coriander
grated rind of ½ lime
2 dried chilies, seeded and chopped
2 tablespoons fish sauce
2 teaspoons sugar
2 tablespoons curry paste
½ teaspoon salt

 Serves 4

Curried rice has an appealing and exotic aroma, and beans add color and a contrast of textures. An exception to the classic rule for stir-frying rice, this cooked rice may be stir-fried immediately, without waiting for it to cool. This is a grand rice dish for any meal. ▪

Heat a wok or large frying-pan and add the oil. When moderately hot, add the beans and stir-fry for about 2 minutes. Put in the rice and continue to stir-fry for 3 minutes. Stir in the rest of the ingredients and mix thoroughly. Cook for another 5 minutes, stirring continuously. Turn the mixture onto a plate and serve at once.

JAPANESE RICE WITH ASPARAGUS

2 cups short-grain rice
2⅔ cups chicken or vegetable
    stock
2 tablespoons light soy sauce
1 tablespoon dark soy sauce
⅔ cup sake, rice wine, or dry
    sherry
1 pound fresh asparagus
2 tablespoons peanut oil
¼ teaspoon salt
2 tablespoons water
2 tablespoons finely shredded
    fresh ginger

 *Serves 2 to 4*

This is a traditional Japanese dish, classic in its simplicity. Appealing to the eye as well as the palate, it is so satisfying that it is almost a meal in itself. This dish is based on short-grain rice. You can substitute broccoli or green beans for the asparagus. ■

Cook the rice according to the method given for long-grain rice on page 178, but substitute stock for the water and add the soy sauce and sake.

Cut off the tough ends of the asparagus, then cut the stalks on the diagonal into 3-inch pieces.

Heat a wok or large frying-pan and add the oil. Put in the asparagus pieces and salt and stir-fry for 4 minutes. Remove the asparagus from the wok and let cool.

Fold the asparagus and ginger into the warmed cooked rice and serve.

Pineapple fried rice

1 large fresh pineapple
1 ounce Chinese dried
   mushrooms
2 tablespoons peanut oil
1 small onion, finely chopped
¼ pound Chinese long beans,
   runner beans, or French
   haricot vert, trimmed and
   diced
2 cups long-grain rice, cooked
2 eggs
2 tablespoons dark soy sauce
1 tablespoon fish sauce

Serves 4 to 6

I first enjoyed this unusual rice dish in Hong Kong and only subsequently learned that it is of Thai origin. Thai cooks commonly hollow out the pineapple and fill it with fried rice or some other tasty stuffing. It is a very attractive way to serve fried rice, but hollowing out the fruit takes a little effort and is not to be done everyday. An easier alternative is to cut the pineapple in half lengthways. This attractive dish makes an impressive centerpiece for a special dinner party. ▪

Carefully cut off and save the pineapple top, leaving about 1-inch of the pineapple under the leaves if you want to use the whole shell for serving. Alternatively, you can cut the pineapple in half lengthways after disposing of the top and leaves. Scoop out the inside fruit, leaving the outer shell of the pineapple intact to serve the fried rice. Coarsely chop the pineapple meat, discarding the tough center core.

Soak the dried mushrooms in warm water for 20 minutes until soft. Squeeze the excess liquid from the mushrooms and remove and discard their stalks. Cut the caps into small dice.

Heat a wok or large frying-pan and add the oil. When almost smoking, add the mushrooms, onions, and beans and stir-fry for 1 minute. Mix in the cold cooked rice and stir-fry for 1 minute. Add the eggs, soy sauce, and fish sauce and continue to stir-fry for 5 minutes over high heat. Stir in the chopped pineapple and stir-fry for about 2 minutes. Scoop the mixture into the hollowed-out pineapple shell and replace the top, or pile the mixture into the two halves, and serve the remaining rice on a platter.

SINGAPORE-STYLE LETTUCE AND FRIED RICE

½ ounce Chinese dried
  mushrooms
2 tablespoons peanut oil
4 shallots, sliced
3 garlic cloves, crushed
2 cups long-grain rice, cooked
2 ounces fresh or frozen peas
3 tablespoons finely chopped
  scallions
2 fresh chilies
2 eggs, beaten
3 tablespoons light soy sauce
½ teaspoon salt
¼ teaspoon freshly ground
  black pepper
½ pound iceberg lettuce,
  finely shredded

GARNISH

2 tablespoons finely chopped
  scallions

 Serves 4

This is an easy fried rice dish to make. The chili adds zest and sparkle to the dish, and the lettuce provides a refreshing touch. ■

Soak the dried mushrooms in warm water for 20 minutes until soft. Squeeze the excess liquid from the mushrooms and remove and discard the stalks. Cut the caps into small dice.

Heat a wok or large frying-pan and add the oil. When almost smoking, add the shallots and garlic and stir-fry for 30 seconds. Put in the cold cooked rice and stir-fry for 1 minute, then add the peas, scallions, and chilies and continue to stir-fry for another 3 minutes. Stir in the beaten egg, soy sauce, salt, and pepper and stir-fry for 2 minutes more or until the eggs have set.

Finally, add the lettuce and mix thoroughly. Turn the mixture onto a serving plate and garnish with the scallions. Serve at once.

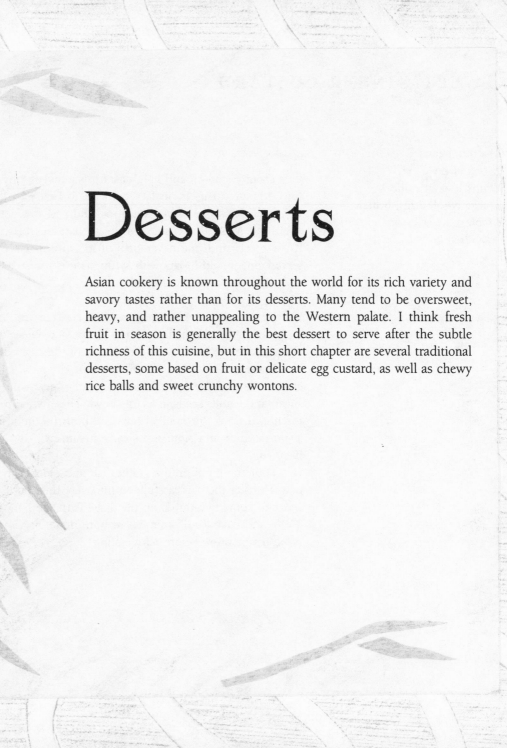

Desserts

Asian cookery is known throughout the world for its rich variety and savory tastes rather than for its desserts. Many tend to be oversweet, heavy, and rather unappealing to the Western palate. I think fresh fruit in season is generally the best dessert to serve after the subtle richness of this cuisine, but in this short chapter are several traditional desserts, some based on fruit or delicate egg custard, as well as chewy rice balls and sweet crunchy wontons.

Sweet ginger custard

2 vanilla beans
½ cup sugar
2 cups low-fat milk
6 large whole eggs, beaten
2 tablespoons finely chopped
  candied ginger

 Serves 10

This creamy smooth and light custard is enlivened by the zest of preserved ginger. This is, in fact, a blend of East and West that works very well. It can be served warm or cold and is a delightful finish to any meal. Make this custard in great quantities because it retains its flavor nicely and one never tires of it. Do not use the Chinese preserved ginger sold in jars with syrup, as it is too strong for this recipe and will overpower the custard. ■

Split the vanilla beans in half and scrape out the seeds with a spoon. Separate the seeds with one tablespoon of the sugar and set aside.

Preheat the oven to 400°F. Combine the milk, vanilla beans, and ginger in a pan and leave it to heat gently. Meanwhile, wisk the eggs, sugar, and vanilla seeds in a large bowl. Then, when the milk is steaming hot, discard the vanilla beans and pour the milk into the egg and sugar mixture in a slow and steady stream, wisking until thoroughly blended.

Pour the liquid into a gratin dish and place it in a large roasting pan. Transfer the pan carefully to the oven, then pour in sufficient hot water to come two-thirds up the dish. Turn the temperature down to 350°F and bake for 45 minutes or until done. Serve warm, or cool to room temperature before refrigerating.

Cold honeydew dessert soup

4 tablespoons small pearl
   tapioca
⅔ cup water
1 ripe honeydew melon,
   about 4 pounds
2⅔ cups fresh or canned
   coconut milk (page 20)
6 tablespoons sugar

 Serves 6 to 8

I first sampled this delicious dessert at the Sichuan Garden Restaurant in Hong Kong. It is suffused with the tastes, fragrances, textures, and colors popular in Southeast Asia. While, here in the West, we tend to prefer the firm white meat of mature coconuts, in Asia, the slightly green or immature coconut is preferred. The meat is quite soft, like a jelly, and can be scooped out with a spoon or one's fingers. The liquid from such coconuts is also rather sweet. Mature coconuts are sweet too, especially when combined with milk and melon. The tapioca adds body to the soup and the result is an unusually refreshing dessert, perfect after any meal. ▪

Combine the tapioca and water in a small bowl and let sit for 45 minutes.

Cut the honeydew melon into quarters, remove the seeds, and cut off the peel. Cut the melon into large pieces. Purée the meat in a blender to a thick liquid consistency. Pour into a medium-sized bowl and refrigerate.

Place the coconut milk in a saucepan, add the sugar and tapioca and simmer for 5 minutes or until it thickens. Allow it to cool, then refrigerate.

When you are ready to serve the soup, pour the two separate mixtures into a large serving bowl, stir well, and serve.

Sweet wontons

1 package wonton skins
   (about 30 to 35 skins)
2 cups peanut oil for deep
   frying
Powdered sugar, for dusting

FILLING

½ cup sultanas or raisins
¼ cup shredded unsweetened
   coconut
⅓ cup walnuts, shelled
2 tablespoons sugar
grated rind of one lemon
1 egg, beaten

 Makes about 30 to 35 wontons

In China, these wontons are called firecrackers because of their shape. This recipe is my variation on that popular Chinese theme. Instead of the traditional stuffing of dates, I use sultanas or raisins combined with shredded unsweetened coconut and walnuts. The result is a sweet, crunchy, and delectable dessert. They may be cooked hours in advance but are tastiest when eaten warm. These wontons are quite addictive. ■

Combine the filling ingredients together in a large bowl and mix well. Then, using a teaspoon, put a small amount of filling in the corner of each wonton skin. Roll it diagonally halfway to the center, pinch down the sides around the filling, wet the corner with water, and fold over to seal well. Gently twist the ends to make an attractive decorative package like a firecracker.

Heat the oil in a deep-fat fryer or large wok until hot. Deep-fry the filled wontons in several batches until they are golden brown, about 3 to 5 minutes. Remove the cooked wontons with a slotted spoon and drain on paper towel. Dust lightly with powdered sugar and serve warm or at room temperature.

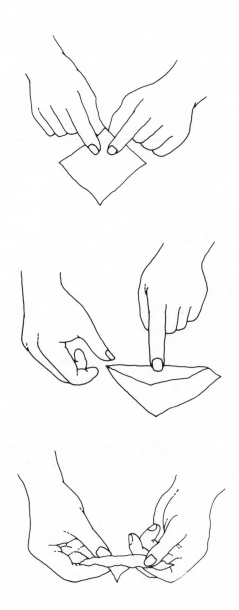

Malaysian coconut custard

4 eggs, beaten
½ cup sugar
2 cups fresh or canned
  coconut milk (page 20)
¼ teaspoon salt

GARNISH
½ cup shredded unsweetened
  coconut

 Serves 6 to 8

Custards are well known around the world, but coconut custard is specifically Thai and Malaysian in origin. In these countries it is usually steamed, but I find it even better cooked in the traditional Western manner, in a hot water bath in the oven. The rich coconut flavor permeates the custard, making it a perfect dessert served hot or cold. Make it in individual ½ cup ramekins if you can. ■

Combine the eggs, sugar, coconut milk, and salt in a large bowl and mix well.

Preheat the oven to 300°F.

Pour the custard mixture into individual ramekins or a large baking dish. Place the ramekins or dish inside a large roasting pan. Transfer the pan carefully to the oven, then pour in sufficient hot water to come two-thirds up the sides of the dishes or dish. Bake for 35 minutes if you are using ramekins, or 1 hour if you are using a large baking dish. You can test if the custard is done by inserting the blade of a knife into the center of the custard. When the custard is done, the blade will come out clean.

Cool and chill the custard until you are ready to serve it. Lightly brown the coconut in a frying-pan over moderate heat. Allow it to cool, then sprinkle the coconut over the top of the custard and serve.

CHINESE TOFFEE APPLES

2 medium firm apples
Juice from 1 lemon
¼ cup cornstarch
2 cups peanut oil, for deep-
frying
1 cup sugar
2 cups water
2 tablespoons white sesame
seeds
Iced water

 Serves 4

There are many versions of this well-known Chinese dessert. I like this one, which I learned in Hong Kong, because it is easy to make. Instead of having to prepare a batter, the apples are simply rolled in cornstarch. Some dexterity is required, but that will come with practice, and these apples are so good you will find yourself practicing a great deal. I would suggest making it for family consumption a few times before trying it for special guests. ■

Peel and core the apples and cut each into 8 large wedges. Mix with the lemon juice to prevent them from browning. Sprinkle the apple wedges with the cornstarch until well coated.

Heat the oil in a deep-fat fryer or wok until moderately hot. Lift out several pieces of apple at a time and shake off any excess cornstarch. Deep-fry for 2 minutes or until golden. Remove with a slotted spoon and drain on paper towel. Repeat the process until you have deep-fried all the apples.

Combine the sugar and water in a pan. Heat the mixture until the sugar melts and begins to caramelize. Turn the heat to *very* low and watch carefully to prevent the syrup from burning.

Just before serving, prepare a bowl of iced water filled with ice cubes. Reheat the oil to moderate and deep-fry the apples a second time for about 2 minutes. Drain again on paper towel. Add the sesame seeds to the caramel syrup and stir. Gently add the fried apples to the syrup to coat. Remove with a slotted spoon and put the coated pieces into the iced water to harden. Do a few at a time to prevent them from sticking together. Remove from the water and place on a serving platter. Serve at once.

RICE PUFFS WITH PRUNE FILLING

1 cup glutinous rice flour
1¼ cups hot water
14 prunes
3 tablespoons white sesame
    seeds
2 cups peanut oil, for deep-
    frying

 Makes about 14 rice balls

These sweet rice balls are a satisfying snack or dessert. They were a favorite treat when I was a boy, with their chewy texture and sweet center. My mother made them with a filling of sweet date paste, but I find that prunes are just as satisfying. The rice balls will puff up and split slightly as they are heated, but don't worry as they will retain their shape and centers. ■

First make the dough. Put the rice flour in a large bowl and gradually stir in the hot water, mixing it all the while with a fork or with chopsticks until most of the water is incorporated. The mixture will be quite sticky. Remove the mixture from the bowl and knead it with your hands until smooth, dusting it from time to time to keep the dough from sticking. This should take about 5 to 6 minutes. Put the dough back into the bowl, cover it with a clean, dry towel, and let it rest for about 30 minutes.

While the dough is resting, pit the prunes.

After the resting period, take the dough out of the bowl and knead it again for about 2 minutes, dusting it with a little rice flour if sticky. Once the dough is smooth, form it into a roll about 9 inches long and about 1 inch in diameter. Take a knife and cut the roll into about 14 equal pieces.

Roll each of the dough pieces into a small round pancake about 3 inches in diameter. Put a prune in the center of each pancake and bring up the sides, pinching the edges to seal well. Roll it into a ball and sprinkle with sesame seeds. Transfer the finished balls to a floured tray and keep them covered until you have filled all the balls in this way.

Heat the oil in a deep-fat fryer or wok until hot. Deep-fry the rice balls in several batches until golden, about 5 minutes. The rice balls will puff up and they may split slightly popping and splattering fat, so stand well back. Remove with a slotted spoon and drain them on paper towel. Serve them at once.

Indonesian fried bananas

3 ripe bananas
¼ cup all-purpose flour
⅔ cup water
1 egg, beaten
2 tablespoons sugar
2 cups peanut oil, for deep-frying
Powdered sugar, for dusting

 Serves 2

This naturally sweet and tasty desert is based on an Indonesian recipe but is actually a common Southeast Asian treat. It is easy to make and the number of portions may be doubled or tripled. ■

Peel the bananas and cut them in half widthwise. For the batter, combine the flour, sugar, egg, and water in a small bowl. Mix them well to form a smooth, thick batter.

Heat the oil in a deep-fat fryer or wok until moderately hot. Put the banana halves into the batter mixture, then lift out the fruit using a slotted spoon and drain off any excess batter. Deep-fry each piece for about 2 minutes until golden and crispy. Remove with a slotted spoon and drain on paper towel. Repeat the process until you have fried all the bananas. Arrange them on a serving platter and dust them with sugar. Serve at once.

Banana crisps

3 firm bananas
2 cups peanut oil, for deep-
    frying
Powdered sugar, for dusting

 Serves 4

This is a popular Thai dessert or snack. The bananas must be sliced *very* thinly by hand, not with a food processor. Buy the firmest ones you can find. Indonesians normally use green, underripe bananas which are easier to slice. Remember that the crisps continue to cook after being removed from the oil, so you must not leave them in too long. The sugar in the bananas caramelizes as they cool. Your touch with this recipe will improve as you master the method. Once the fried banana slices have cooled thoroughly, they become quite crispy. Serve warm or cold. ■

Peel and slice the bananas into very thin rounds.

Heat the oil in a deep-fat fryer or wok until hot. Fry several slices of the banana at a time for 2 to 3 minutes, or until they are a deep golden brown, taking care not to burn them. Drain on paper towel and allow to cool.

Dust them lightly with sugar and serve.

Recipes for Special Occasions

LIGHT AND SUMMERY RECIPES

Perfect for warm weather, these dishes are light and refreshing and can accompany richer vegetarian or meat dishes. Many of them are equally delicious served at room temperature, making them ideal for summer indoor or outdoor dining. The vegetables used make the most of summer's fresh harvest. Mix and match these recipes with your favorite foods.

- Crunchy Radish Salad
- Eggplant with Sesame Sauce
- Japanese-Style Marinated Mushrooms
- Tangy Tomato Soup with Lemongrass
- Hot and Sour Cucumber Salad
- Spicy Citrus-Flavored Noodles
- Homemade Chinese Rice "Fun" Noodles with Peppers
- Fresh Pasta with Coriander, Ginger, and Basil Pesto

Do-ahead recipes

These recipes can be partially or entirely made ahead of time. Essential for today's busy life-style, they can save time without compromising quality and taste.

- Vietnamese-Style Vegetarian Spring Rolls
- Northern Chinese Vegetable Potstickers (can be frozen)
- Chinese Pancakes (can be frozen)
- Sweet Wontons
- Spicy Korean Kimchi
- Sugar Walnuts
- Hot and Spicy Walnuts
- Indonesian Cauliflower Soup
- Peppery Eggplant
- Cold Green Bean Salad
- Asparagus with Tangy Mustard Dressing
- Singapore-Style Rice Noodles
- Cold Honeydew Dessert Soup
- Sweet Ginger Custard
- Malaysian Coconut Custard

COMFORTING FOODS FOR COLD NIGHTS

Hearty and filling vegetarian dishes can be comforting and satisfying on cold nights, as these recipes illustrate. Many of them are spicy—so they warm the palate as well as the body.

- Winter Vegetable Fritters

- Fiery Sichuan Soup

- Coconut-Stewed Bean Curd and Vegetables

- Fragrant Coconut Rice

- Scallion Pancakes

- Chinese Rice Porridge with Condiments

- Northern Chinese Vegetable Potstickers

- Tan Tan Noodles

- Home-Style Spicy Bean Curd

COMPLICATED RECIPES MADE EASY

These are recipes which require a bit of work. I have discovered they are fun to prepare when your family or guests pitch in to help. It is a congenial way to enjoy lengthy preparations and many people love to help. Make sure that you direct the process very carefully.

- Vietnamese-Style Vegetarian Spring Rolls
- Northern Chinese Vegetarian Potstickers
- Crispy Vegetarian Wontons
- Scallion Pancakes
- Vegetable Medley with Tomato-Garlic Sauce
- Stuffed Bean Curd Squares
- Fragrant Rice Noodle Salad
- Sweet Wontons
- Chinese Toffee Apples
- Rice Puffs with Prune Filling
- Banana Crisps

Frugal vegetarian recipes

These recipes use inexpensive ingredients, especially if you shop seasonally. They are substantial and delicious.

- Udon Noodles in Broth
- Vegetarian Chow Mein
- Thai Corn Pancakes
- Scallion Pancakes
- Crunchy Radish Salad
- Indonesian Cauliflower Soup
- Fragrant Noodle Soup
- Hot and Sour Cucumber Salad
- Cold Green Bean Salad
- Stir-fried Spicy Carrots
- Stir-fried Lettuce
- Bean Curd Custard in Oyster Sauce
- Spinach and Rice Noodles
- Singapore-Style Lettuce Fried Rice
- Chinese Toffee Apples

RECIPES FOR LARGE CROWDS

These dishes can be easily doubled or tripled. Many of them are ideal for a buffet. Some can be served at room temperature, which is helpful when entertaining.

- Rainbow Vegetables in Lettuce Cups
- Vegetable Medley with Tomato-Garlic Sauce
- Southeast Asian Noodle Salad
- Pineapple Fried Rice
- Japanese-Style Marinated Mushrooms
- Sesame Buckwheat Noodles
- Cold Sichuan Noodles
- Cold Honeydew Dessert Soup

One-dish Meals or Quick Dinners in Minutes

Today there is rarely time to prepare elaborate multi-dish meals, so I find the following recipes perfect for hearty and satisfying one-dish meals with lots of flavors and tastes. Single recipes can be prepared in minutes, and with one or two recipes, you can compose a delicious, healthy meal in less than an hour.

- Coconut-Stewed Bean Curd and Vegetables
- Crispy Cantonese-Style Noodles with Vegetables
- Stir-fried Vegetables over a Rice Noodle Cloud
- Southeast Asian Vegetable Soup
- Curried Fried Rice with Green Beans
- Soft Bean Curd and Spinach Soup
- Spinach in Oyster Sauce
- Asparagus with Tangy Mustard Dressing
- Crispy Scallion Omelette
- Sesame Buckwheat Noodles

ELEGANT AND EASY RECIPES

These recipes are ideal for dinner parties, complementing more complicated courses. They look elegant but are easy to make. Their sophisticated flavors give a cosmopolitan touch to your dinner menu —be it East or West.

- Sugar Walnuts

- Crispy Vegetarian Wontons

- Sizzling Rice Soup

- Asparagus with Tangy Mustard Dressing

- East-West Shredded Salad

- Spinach and Egg-Ribbon Soup

- Mock Vegetable Pasta

- Summer Pepper Stir-fry

- Fragrant Coconut Rice

- Bean Sprout Salad

- Malaysian Coconut Custard

VEGETARIAN DISHES TO ACCOMPANY BARBECUES

These recipes are a perfect foil for the popular, traditional American barbecue. Many of them are great counterpoints to the smoky flavor of barbecued foods. And they are quick and easy to make—in keeping with the casual warm weather cooking. They add color and exotic flavors to your barbecues.

- Crunchy Radish Salad

- Creamy Eggplant and Tomato Soup

- Green and White Jade Salad

- Spinach in Oyster Sauce

- Grilled Mushrooms with Lemon Sauce

- Southeast Asian Noodle Salad

- Japanese Rice with Asparagus

- Grilled Bean Curd Shish Kebabs

Shopping Guide

I have designed this index to be a handy shopping and cooking guide. It does not include all the recipes in the book, and it does not include recipes that call for several different vegetables. Check the recipe before shopping to see that you have the other ingredients you may need.

⊡ **ASPARAGUS**
Asparagus with Tangy Mustard Dressing
Stir-fried Asparagus in Black Bean Sauce
Asparagus with Chinese Black Mushrooms
Japanese Rice with Asparagus

⊡ **BEAN CURD**
See Chapter 5

⊡ **BEAN SPROUTS**
Stir-fried "Silver Sprouts"
Bean Sprout Salad

⊡ **BEANS**
Cold Green Bean Salad
Green Beans in Pungent Sauce
Curried Fried Rice with Green Beans

⊡ **BITTER MELON**
Bitter Melon with Black Bean Sauce

- **BROCCOLI** Dry-Braised Bamboo Shoots with Broccoli
  Hong Kong–Style Fried Rice

- **CARROTS** Stir-fried Spicy Carrots

- **CAULIFLOWER** Indonesian Cauliflower Soup
  Green and White Jade Salad

- **CHINESE CABBAGE** Spicy Korean Kimchi
  Savory Bean Curd Casserole

- **CORN** Thai Corn Pancakes
  Corn and Ginger Soup
  Corn and Ginger Fried Rice

- **CUCUMBERS** Hot and Sour Cucumber Salad
  Stir-fried Cucumbers
  Cucumber Noodle Salad

- **EGGPLANT** Eggplants with Sesame Sauce
  Creamy Eggplant and Tomato Soup
  Peppery Eggplant
  Chinese Eggplant Salad
  Sichuan Fried Eggplant

- **LEEKS** Pan-fried Bean Curd with Leeks

- **LETTUCE (ICEBERG)** East-West Shredded Salad
  Stir-fried Lettuce
  Singapore-Style Lettuce Fried Rice

- **MUSHROOMS** Two Mushroom Rice

Chinese black mushrooms

Asparagus with Chinese Black Mushrooms
Eggs with Chinese Mushrooms
Braised Chinese Mushrooms

Fresh mushrooms

Button Mushrooms in Oyster Sauce
Grilled Mushrooms with Lemon Sauce
Cold Chinese Noodle Salad with Mushrooms

Fungus

Cloud Ears in Hoisin Sauce
Cloud Ears Stir-fried with Snow Peas

⊡ **NOODLES**

Bean thread (transparent) noodles

Savory Bean Curd Casserole
Spicy Bean Thread Noodles with Dried Shrimp
Korean Bean Thread Sesame Noodles with Vegetables

Buckwheat

Sesame Buckwheat Noodles

Rice noodles

Crispy Noodle Salad
Light and Easy Rice Noodles
Homemade Chinese Fresh Rice "Fun" Noodles
Homemade Chinese Rice "Fun" Noodles with Peppers
Singapore-Style Rice Noodles
Southeast Asian Noodle Salad
Spinach and Rice Noodles
Fragrant Rice Noodle Salad

Egg noodles

Tan Tan Noodles
Spicy Black Bean Sauce Noodles
Fresh Pasta with Coriander, Ginger, and Basil Pesto
Singapore Noodles
Vegetarian Chow Mein
Hot and Sour Noodles
Spicy Citrus-Flavored Noodles
Cold Curry-Flavored Noodles
Cold Sichuan Noodles
Cold Chinese Noodle Salad with Mushrooms
Crispy Cantonese-Style Noodles with Vegetables

Udon

Udon Noodles in Broth

☐ **PEPPERS**

Homemade Chinese Rice "Fun" Noodles with Peppers
Summer Pepper Stir-fry
Rainbow Vegetables in Lettuce Cups

☐ **RADISH**

Steamed Vegetable Soup
Crunchy Radish Salad

☐ **RICE**

See Chapter 8

☐ **SCALLIONS**

Scallion Pancakes
Crispy Scallion Omelette

☐ **SNOW PEAS**

Cloud Ears Stir-fried with Snow Peas

☐ **SPINACH**

Soft Bean Curd and Spinach Soup
Spinach and Egg-Ribbon Soup
Spinach in Oyster Sauce
Sesame-Dressed Spinach Salad
Spinach and Rice Noodles

☐ **ZUCCHINI**

Mock Vegetable Pasta

Index

About the Author

Ken Hom is described by Craig Claiborne, food editor of *The New York Times,* as "one of the world's greatest authorities on Chinese cooking." Paul Levy, food and wine editor of *The Observor,* calls him "a genuinely brilliant, natural, and intuitive cook, and the dishes that result from this combining of cuisines are unforced and appetizing." He presented the highly acclaimed BBC series *Chinese Cookery* (shown on public television in this country) and the best-selling book (Harper & Row) which accompanied the series.

Born in America, Ken Hom speaks several languages, studied medieval art history, and was formerly a professional photographer and free-lance television producer. He has traveled extensively throughout the world and lived in Europe, where he studied film.

His cooking school in Hong Kong, where he conducts classes each year, has received wide international acclaim and a following among many food professionals. He currently writes and consults on food for many magazines and companies throughout the world. He is the author of the critically acclaimed *Ken Hom's East Meets West Cuisine* and co-authored the highly regarded *Chinese Technique* (both published by Simon & Schuster). Ken Hom now lives in Berkeley, California, and in Paris, France.